KILLER
CATCHERS

ANDY OWENS AND
CHRIS ELLIS

KILLER CATCHERS

FOURTEEN TRUE STORIES
OF HOW BRITAIN'S WICKEDEST
MURDERERS WERE BROUGHT
TO JUSTICE.

JOHN BLAKE

Published by John Blake Publishing Ltd,
3 Bramber Court, 2 Bramber Road,
London W14 9PB, England

www.blake.co.uk

First published in paperback in 2008

ISBN: 978 1 84454 503 2

British Library Cataloguing-in-Publication Data:

A catalogue record for this book is available from the British Library.

Design by www.envydesign.co.uk

Printed in the UK by CPI Bookmarque, Croydon, CR0 4TD

1 3 5 7 9 10 8 6 4 2

Papers used by John Blake Publishing are natural, recyclable products made from wood grown in sustainable forests. The manufacturing processes conform to the environmental regulations of the country of origin.

Dedication:

(from Chris Ellis)
To my beautiful wife Julie and our children
Jodie, Connor and Brandon

(from Andy Owens)
For my dad – the late Jack Owens – a West Yorkshire
police constable for over thirty years.

ACKNOWLEDGEMENTS

The authors would like to thank Paul Williams for his brilliant and highly recommended research service www.murderfiles.com; Terry Hayden for the extensive and well-researched information on his excellent website www.murderuk.com; Tony Youens, Adrian Shaw and Tony Batters for their painstaking research on the Ruark case, detailed in the chapter *Life After Death* (for information on this and other fascinating research by Mr Youens see www.tonyyouens.com).

Particular thanks to Detective Chief Superintendent Brian Taylor and Police Constable Eddie Gorny – both of West Yorkshire Police – for taking time to help us with our research for the chapter 'Ten Minutes of Madness'. Their comments gave the authors a valuable insight into – and appreciation of – the commitment, determination and professionalism of our British police forces when faced with investigating such horrific cases. It showed us that, while the law courts often forget the victims and their families, the police never do.

Andy Owens and Chris Ellis

CONTENTS

1

TEN MINUTES OF MADNESS

The eager young policeman stepped into the River Aire and immediately felt the chilly water soak through his trousers and seep into his boots.

A local woman had seemingly vanished on her way to work along the towpath of the Leeds–Liverpool Canal the previous evening, and a Missing Persons report had been filed. Although a team of police officers had been despatched immediately, the search was hampered by the darkness and the officers failed to find any trace of her.

Next morning, 23-year-old Eddie Gorny and other officers beginning the 6.00am shift resumed the search and were deployed to various points along the 600-yard walk between her home in Shipley, West Yorkshire, and Salts Mill, at Saltaire, where she was employed.

Although it was the last day of August 1977, the morning was already light as PC Gorny searched the

Coach Road side of the River Aire. He scanned the reeds that skirted the riverbank for some trace of the missing woman. And it was at that moment that he glimpsed something in the water.

Drawing closer, he could see it looked like a handbag, but it wasn't until he had waded in further to reach it that he realised its owner could be close by – and probably in the river. Reaching into the bag, he found a letter with the name 'Mary Gregson' written on it.

Peering further downstream, something else caught his eye, something so horrible that the young constable – just fresh from police training, on the first few days of his beat – would remember it for many years to come.

Something was sticking out of the water at an awkward angle. It was a woman's arm ...

The sun had been shining that previous evening, as 39-year-old Mary Gregson left her pretty canal-side cottage at Jane Hills, Shipley, where she had lived for 14 years with her husband Bill and their young son.

The couple married in 1959, and they ran a fish and chip shop together in Shipley, before Mary left to work at a chemist. She gave up her job in 1966 to have their son, Michael, and then returned to work as a full-time cleaner in 1976. After recovering from a serious illness, she continued as a part-time cleaner, while Bill worked full-time at a factory in nearby Bingley.

That evening, she left the couple's cottage to walk the 600 yards to Salts Mill, to cover for a friend who had broken her ankle. Mary had arranged to meet a colleague near the canal towpath bridge, not far from her home – but never arrived.

Her 11-year-old son, Michael, was one of the last people

to see her alive. He can still recall that final memory of his mother as she turned slightly, said 'Ta-ra,' and was gone.

When her workmate finished her shift at 7.30pm that evening, she called round to Mary's cottage to ask why her colleague had not turned up for work. But all she found was Mary's confused and worried husband, Bill, becoming increasingly anxious for her safety, calling friends and relatives about her disappearance – and then the police.

The next day, following PC Gorny's discovery, police recovered Mary Gregson's badly bruised body from the River Aire, which runs adjacent to the Leeds–Liverpool Canal.

At this point, her name was not released to the press. A brief entry on page 11 of that evening's edition of the *Telegraph & Argus*, titled 'MYSTERY OF BODY FOUND IN RIVER', appealing for information from the public, offered a brief description of the dead woman, '... about 40 years old ...[she was] wearing a blue anorak with thin red stripes, blue jeans, moccasin shoes [and] carrying a blue shoulder bag'.

However, it quickly became evident that she had been murdered. A post-mortem, attended by murder detectives and PC Gorny, showed that, although Mrs Gregson had put up a fight, she stood little chance against her killer.

She had been the victim of a brutal attack, during which she had been slapped and punched, pulled down the grass bank from the canal towpath to the edge of the River Aire, sexually assaulted and her head had been repeatedly struck on the ground. Then her killer had kneeled on her chest, strangled her with a ligature, then finally dumped her body in the water.

As the body had been in the river overnight, attempts

to carry out tests on Mrs Gregson's clothing proved largely unsuccessful. The dirty river water meant that precious evidence had been contaminated, but forensic scientists discovered a small amount of the murderer's semen.

While scientists beavered away in the lab, the police began interviewing thousands of local residents and employees.

The profile of the killer, issued by the then senior investigating officer, Detective Chief Superintendent John Domaille, was very basic – a white man aged between 16 and 40. This motivated police first to interview the 800 workers on the nearby Laing building site, where the new Inland Revenue office was being constructed, partly because of the close proximity to where Mrs Gregson's body had been found, but also because most of the men fitted this profile.

Police appealed for witnesses to come forward, which resulted in them being approached by an Italian woman who, speaking in broken English, explained how she had approached a man she had seen standing over Mrs Gregson's body and spoke to him.

The witness was able to give police a more detailed description of him: white, in his mid-20s, around 5ft 10in tall, with a long face, gormless expression, thin nose and light brown hair. He even told her his name. He said it was 'Jan' – presumably pronounced with a 'Y'. This was surprising because, as it turned out, the killer had obviously told her his real name, which was then mispronounced by the foreign witness. With the benefit of hindsight, people may ask why the police did not act upon this information, but the witness who was interviewed by police – and had an Italian priest at her side as an interpreter – was adamant the man's name was either Jan or Janny.

When the witness questioned 'Jan', the latter told her he thought that the woman had fallen. The witness then hurried off and approached several other passers-by. Some of these people went to the spot where Jan had been seen, but there was no sign of him or the woman anywhere. Of course, by this time, the killer had no doubt disposed of his victim in the river and fled the scene.

Although several artists' impressions were drawn up, none was ever released to the public. Why? At the time, an artist's impression of the man wanted by police in connection with the Yorkshire Ripper case had resulted in thousands of people phoning the police to report their suspicions about someone, simply because he had a beard! The already exhaustive manpower being invested into the Gregson case could have doubled or even tripled if a similar photo-fit had been issued about Mary's killer. This partly influenced the police's decision not to release the impression to the public.

DCS Brian Taylor disclosed another reason to the authors. 'If someone thought they recognised the verbal description of the suspect released by police, they may have been put off from calling detectives about their suspicions, perhaps because the person in mind may bear little or no resemblance to the photo-fit impression. We have to be very careful about what we release to the public. All factors need to be taken into consideration.'

Just 16 days after the murder, police staged a reconstruction, in an effort to jog people's memories.

Nineteen-year-old WPC Jill Broadhead, who had joined the force only a few days before the murder, volunteered to retrace the steps of Mrs Gregson, leaving the family's canal-side cottage as she had done on that fateful evening.

Although the police thought it better that the victim's son did not take part, 11-year-old Michael insisted on doing so, 'for the sake of his mum', according to the police.

At 5.20pm, WPC Broadhead left the cottage to walk to Salts Mill, and, 25 minutes later, Bill Gregson rode past on his bicycle as he had done on the day of the murder, and other people who had contacted the police repeated their own movements at the time. Several key witnesses, including a man seen walking over a bridge spanning the River Aire, who had failed to come forward despite a widespread police appeal, were played by members of the force.

Despite having received national coverage for the reconstruction, no new serious leads were forthcoming.

Back at the forensic laboratory, the first attempt to attract DNA had proved unsuccessful. In hindsight, the original method proved comparatively primitive to today's techniques; it didn't even provide detectives with the killer's blood group.

By January 1978, having interviewed over 9,000 construction workers, employees at Salts Mill and countless local residents, investing over 40,000 hours of investigations, the police had found nothing significant, so the case was filed, pending further developments.

Detective Inspector Chris Wilson, who was involved in the case until he retired in 1998, said he felt that one day scientists would find the right way to extract DNA from Mrs Gregson's clothing. Both the police and the Gregson family firmly believed that the killer would be caught; they just had to wait for science to show them the way.

'The case was never closed,' DCS Brian Taylor told the journal *Police Review*. 'It was put on ice, into deep-freeze if you like, should something come along.'

He was among several detectives who always kept in close contact with the family and often visited Bill and Michael Gregson. Detective Inspector Chris Wilson recalled that, on his visits, Bill would always answer the door expectantly.

'I could see his face. I could see it in his eyes, that he thought I was going to tell him we had caught the fellow. When you told him you were just calling in, his face sank.' Some of the detectives told of how they felt they were letting everybody down, yet remained confident that, one day, they would apprehend the person responsible.

Of course, the murder affected the whole family. Michael Gregson can still not bring himself to talk publicly about the death of his mother. Mary's parents began to suffer from heart problems soon after the murder, and have both since died. One of Mary's sisters, Mrs Judith Sykes, said, 'It just changed our lives altogether. I remember for a long time not feeling in total control. The stress and tension for all of us was just incredible. I used to walk around Shipley and Saltaire looking at people and thinking, Is it you? Do you know something? It wasn't a proper existence.'

But it was Bill Gregson, perhaps more than anyone, who was most affected. DI Wilson told how the father and widower was in constant torment. 'Not just for the first few weeks, but for years afterwards.' Mr Gregson had told the detective, 'There hasn't been a day since she died when I haven't had a cry, but I usually do it alone.'

He said that many people walk the canal towpath every

day, and he wondered if he had ever rubbed shoulders with his wife's killer. Although he wanted to see the murderer caught and punished, he also wanted to know his reason for 'snuffing out the life of a lovely wife and mother who never harmed a soul'.

Every morning, Mr Gregson would walk to the spot where his wife had been murdered. He would stand there for a while, feeding the birds, gaining great comfort from that daily visit. 'I know it sounds daft,' he told a local newspaper many years ago, 'but I can feel her spirit there. It is there that we are close again ...'

But tragically, in 1981, just four years after the murder, Bill Gregson collapsed at the same spot and died of a heart-attack. He was just 54.

DCS Taylor recalls how they revisited the case, in 1988, due to a possible breakthrough.

A man was being investigated for a robbery and, as always when a crime with the same characteristics comes to the attention of the police, they thought, Could he have killed Mary Gregson? The robber used to walk the canal towpath, near to where Mary Gregson lived, and he and his family had connections to Saltaire village. Also, he was a man who had used violence against people and had previous convictions for sexual offences. So the theory fitted rather neatly.

The science of DNA profiling had come a long way in the 11 years since the Mary Gregson murder. The new technique of MLP (multi-locus probing) was far more advanced than earlier tests, so a new extraction and analysis was carried out on the semen stain from the victim's underwear, to see if it would match the profile of the robber.

But the new MLP technique did not prove to be sufficiently advanced to provide a profile. Although devised three years earlier in 1985, it still required a large amount of biological material to produce a profile. So the exhibits and documents were stored away again, safely under lock and key.

Four years later, in 1992, DI Chris Binns – then a detective constable – contacted DCS Taylor about a new improved technique – SLP (single-locus probing) – that had been subsequently developed as a more sensitive replacement for MLP, and the two detectives thought they should test it again. Again, an anxious wait followed, but they still could not produce a profile of the killer. Again, they locked away the clothing and other exhibits and held their breaths for further developments. The detectives paid close attention to the steady advances and were always keen to read the latest newsletters from the DNA laboratories. One in particular, six years after the last breakthrough, referred to a test termed the DNA LCN (Low Copy Number) technique, which follows on from the routine SGM*plus*™ (Single Generation Multiplex) profiling technique.

The FSS (Forensic Science Services) stated that, 'LCN is a super-sensitive technique, which can produce DNA profiles from very small amounts of DNA. It has the potential to produce a DNA profile from samples where other previous techniques have failed, or from samples that would not be suitable from standard DNA testing.'

The super-sensitivity of DNA LCN allows the FSS to target tiny areas on items where an offender is believed to have transferred DNA through touch, such as the possible residue from skin cells or sweat that might be found in a fingerprint. Profiles using this technique have been successfully mapped from items such as discarded tools, matchsticks and weapon handles.

The DNA samples taken from Mary Gregson's clothing had all been used up. MLP and SLP analyses had depleted the sample and had come up with nothing. So the FSS went back to the exhibit again and again, searching fibre by fibre and, eventually, found microscopic samples of semen.

Scientists at the lab in Wetherby did the initial work, which extracted the DNA samples, and then the FSS laboratory in Birmingham did further work. The team found that they were able to use the sample to create a definitive DNA profile of the murder suspect. Success at last!

Now, the chances of someone sharing the same profile as that of the suspect were one in a billion, whereas with previous techniques the odds were one in 50 million.

Dr Jonathan Whitaker, who gave police the DNA profile of the killer, said, 'LCN is the most sensitive service and achieves outstanding results. It gives us an opportunity to get a result from just a few cells or old degraded samples.' The DNA profile could now be drawn from minute evidence such as dried-up blood or semen – or even a speck of dandruff.

When DCS Brian Taylor reopened the investigation, the mood was optimistic. Once the killer's DNA profile had been drawn up, it was compared to the national DNA database, but no match was found against the 750,000 existing criminal profiles.

So police knew they had to begin from scratch and devise a testing programme. They launched a nationwide appeal and called in a criminal profiler to produce a psycho-fit – a psychological profile of the killer.

The psychologist suggested that the killer, who would now be in his mid-40s, may have come from a poor background, perhaps been abused as a child, and had committed other crimes.

DCS Brian Taylor who led the reopened inquiry, appealed for local people to cast their minds back and report any suspicions they may have had at the time of the murder or since – and also ask friends and relatives to do the same. He said he was aware of the impact the murder had had on the town and that local people discussed the subject, even after all this time.

He said, 'We need to trace anyone we spoke to and who may have moved away from the area or anyone who wasn't interviewed at the time. The majority of the original interviewees will still be living in the vicinity, but, over 22 years, people tend to move away or even emigrate.

'I now have the scientific means to eliminate people from the inquiry. All but one person is innocent of the crime and I finally have the facility to prove that.'

He allayed fears from anyone who was sceptical of the chances of error with this new technique. 'There is only one person who needs to be afraid,' he said. 'And that is the killer of Mary Gregson. Now that we have a definite DNA profile, this makes the murder a highly detectable offence. We can quickly tell whether someone is guilty or innocent.'

It was reported at the time that the planned mass screening of the original 4,000 'suspects' was set to take two years to complete – and, if no DNA match was established with any of them, the case was likely to be shelved once more.

Although the DNA breakthrough had made it possible to re-open the inquiry, the real detective work had just begun. At the time, DCS Taylor said, 'Just because we have a profile of the killer, it doesn't solve the case – it merely gives us the means to solve it.'

The police now had to trace 2,500 people out of the original 9,000 interviewees who, in 1977, fitted the parameters of the profile – a white man aged 16 to 40.

'What you don't do is say, "I'm going to find all the men who fitted that age group and test them all." That would take months and, after 2,000, you may find that the second person you tested was the one who matched the profile.

'So we started up a production-line system. A points system was applied. First of all, we wanted to take a sample of all the builders who had been working on the Laing construction site. But there were 800 of them. Who do you test first?'

The scoring system was based on a number of factors: did the person know Mary Gregson; had the person ever visited the scene itself; what convictions, if any, did he have?

'It wasn't random,' said the senior detective. 'It was part of a pre-determined investigative strategy, and we systematically worked our way through that strategy.

'It was then necessary to trace those that we swabbed. Many had moved away, so police officers had painstakingly and laboriously to trace them all. The eight detectives travelled from the south coast of England to the very north of Scotland. We had a hired car and that car travelled 20,000 miles. Partnership agencies also assisted, including the armed forces, the Prison Service and Department of Health.'

Officers began working their way through the men who were contacted during the original inquiry, asking each to provide a 'buccal swab' – a swab rubbed on the inside of the cheek – which was then returned to the lab for analysis.

Out of the first 1,000 swabs taken – one match was found. On 5 April, the DNA laboratory at the FSS in Birmingham matched the swab from number 532. It belonged to Ian Richard Lowther, a 47-year-old van driver from the nearby district of Baildon, in Bradford.

On Saturday, 8 April 2000, Lowther answered his door to find a team of Bradford detectives who had come to arrest him 22 years and 211 days after he murdered Mary Gregson. This was the second time in the previous two months that he had been visited by the police, since the reopening of the inquiry. When the police knocked on his door, he didn't seem the slightest bit surprised. He looked like someone who was expecting a second visit. He seemed almost relieved that the burden had finally been lifted.

Just before he accompanied detectives back to the station, he placed his slippers behind the front door as if anticipating his return home. One detective told him that he wouldn't need them again, to which Lowther, meticulous to the end, merely shrugged, saying, 'Everything has a place.'

Once confronted with the DNA evidence, Ian Lowther confessed his guilt. He was never released from custody and, before his final court appearance, he instructed his solicitors to put his house up for sale.

Originally, Lowther had voluntarily given the buccal swab, when police first called round two months earlier in February, and must have known that his secret was about to be discovered. He had seen the re-opening of the inquiry, advertised on BBC's *Crimewatch* programme, a month before, during which another reconstruction was staged, in which DCS Taylor, Mrs Judith Sykes and PC Gorny featured among the interviewees.

Police remembered interviewing Lowther on 2 September 1977, two days after Mrs Gregson's body was found. He was interviewed because he fitted the age parameters and was employed on the Laing building site.

If the LCN technique had been available at the time, Lowther would have been invited to give a buccal swab. 'We would have had him as soon as his profile was obtained,' said DCS Taylor. 'He would have been arrested and charged – there's no doubt about that.'

Ironically, although the search for the killer had stretched right across Britain, the killer had been on their back doorstep all the time, having never moved away from the area – and only a few hundred yards from the spot where he had brutally murdered Mary Gregson.

At the time of the murder, Lowther was 24 years of age, living with his wife and young daughter, and working as a labourer on the construction site. Originally interviewed by police, he said he had heard about the murder on TV and, having been shown a photograph of the victim, said he did not recognise her.

Initially, Lowther claimed to have been working at the time of the murder, but this was later found to be untrue. Questioned a second time, he said he had actually been skiving from work, drinking in the pub, and did not want to get into trouble. As several fellow employees had given similar excuses, the police had no reason to doubt his word. He was also able to convince police that there had been nothing unusual in his movements, as he left the pub that evening to pick up his daughter from his mother-in-law's house.

Although Lowther had not been excluded from the investigation, there was no reason to suspect him of the murder, and he escaped becoming a prime suspect.

The fact is, Lowther had been drinking more than usual. Only a moderate drinker, he had downed seven pints at lunchtime, when he should have been at work. Knowing that it would be better to sober up before picking up his daughter from his mother-in-law's house, he took a walk along the canal towpath for some fresh air. It was a chance meeting with Mary Gregson on her way to work, which led to the events that, ultimately, destroyed many lives.

At the subsequent trial, Simon Lawlor QC, representing Lowther, described the murder as 'ten minutes of total and, it has to be said, brutal madness'.

The murder was initially considered by some to have been committed by the Yorkshire Ripper or some other psychopathic serial killer, but detectives at the time thought it unlikely.

In fact, DCS Taylor told the authors that he considered 'Ten Minutes of Madness' to be an apt title for the chapter. He said that there was a general feeling among detectives during the investigation that the killer was quite a normal person, who had experienced ten minutes of madness, perhaps following a heavy drinking binge. Of course, this was mere speculation and their suspicions were not released to the public.

Friends and relatives of Mary Gregson could not understand why an otherwise quiet family man should suddenly sexually assault and murder a complete stranger. Mrs Gregson's sister, Mrs Judith Sykes, found it utterly baffling. 'I suppose you get a sort of image of the killer in your mind and, when I first saw Lowther in court, I just couldn't believe it. He looked like an ordinary man and, from what I learned about him, it just doesn't make any sense at all. It's all right to say he'd been drinking – but a lot of people go out for a drink and they don't do this.'

Although Lowther appeared in court on 10 April 2000, it wasn't until 29 September that he reappeared to plead guilty and was then sentenced to life imprisonment.

Commenting on the hearing, Mrs Sykes continued, 'Some people might think, Poor soul – he's had one moment of madness and been a good boy ever since ... he's tortured our family for 23 years.'

Lowther told police he had an inaccurate memory of the day of the murder and could still not explain his reasons for approaching Mrs Gregson and his violent reaction to her when his advances were rebuffed. Since the murder, he had been leading a double life, but his conscience did not trouble him enough to go to the police, even though many people in the local community had come under suspicion, including members of the victim's family.

DCS Taylor said, 'The family members weren't prime suspects as such, but you have to bear in mind that 73 per cent of all murders are committed by family members or others known to the victims, and so they, like everyone else, had to be considered before they were eliminated from suspicion. You have to keep a completely open mind about everyone. If you ignore the possibility of a particular person being the killer, then that could mean the difference between solving the case or not.'

Since Lowther's divorce in 1999, when he set up home alone in Derwent Avenue, Baildon, his neighbours said he lived the life of a virtual recluse. He was a quiet man who kept himself to himself. Most of the neighbours never really knew him and never imagined he would be capable of such a brutal act.

Although he didn't use local shops or pubs, he kept himself fit at the local gym.

When the murder investigation reopened, one neighbour said, 'The Gregson murder posters were put up all around this area last year. He must have seen one every day.'

However, neighbours from Central Avenue, where Lowther lived with his wife, painted a very different picture. One of them said, 'There's nothing bad to say about him, other than he's a lovely man. The kids all liked him and we couldn't have wished for a better neighbour. It came as something of a shock when we found out he had been arrested.'

Lowther was born in Harrogate into a respectable middle-class family, and left school at the age of 16 with no qualifications. When he started a three-year apprenticeship at Harrogate Technical College, he was granted a day-release to Shipley College, where he met his future wife, Carol. They married in Harrogate in 1973 and moved to a council flat in Denby Drive, Baildon. Later that year, their only child, Carmen, was born. Three-and-a-half years later, they moved to a larger house in Central Avenue.

In November 1976, John Laing & Co employed Lowther for the building of the new Inland Revenue site in Shipley. While he was working there, he murdered Mary Gregson. Despite police appeals, Lowther slipped through the net and, a few weeks after the murder, he left Laing, and worked in the building trade and as a labourer for several firms in Shipley and Baildon.

At the time of his arrest, he was employed as a delivery driver for a company based in Bradford city centre and was regarded as an excellent and conscientious employee. After the divorce, he bought his last house from his daughter, in Derwent Avenue, where he lived until his arrest. Police described him as a loner and otherwise model citizen. Methodical and meticulous, he was well liked by work colleagues and known as Uncle Ian to his friends' children.

His neighbours recall frequent visits from his daughter and four grandchildren, as he played with them in his small, well-kept back garden. 'He was quiet, but a belting man once you got to know him,' described one neighbour, who often asked him to babysit her children.

His books at home revealed his love of walking in the Dales and it was a particular love of solitude which was partly the reason for the couple's marriage break-up in 1999. It is clear from Lowther's family, friends and neighbours that they had no knowledge or suspicion of his deadly secret.

It is strange, too, how Lowther never moved away from the area, regardless of the terrible memory of what he did all those years ago.

Mary's husband, Bill Gregson, often wondered if he had ever rubbed shoulders with Mary's killer on the busy canal towpath by their home. It is very possible he had done – and perhaps more than once. After the murder, Lowther continued to work at the construction site, only yards from where he murdered Mary Gregson. He must have passed that particular spot hundreds of times.

And this was a particularly chilling aspect of the case. That he could commit such a brutal act of murder for no apparent reason and then continue to live a lie in the immediate neighbourhood for the next 23 years.

DCS Taylor said he found it amazing how Lowther had continued to live so close to the scene of the crime. 'He could have gone to the end of his garden last year [1999] and seen the *Crimewatch* reconstruction. It's pretty unbelievable.'

Living just a mile from the scene of the murder, he had not shown any remorse, or given any explanation as to why he had killed Mary Gregson.

Said the senior detective, 'He is a quiet man who kept himself to himself. He lived an ordered life and was meticulous in his habits. Police described him as a quiet, reserved, nice man. Since the murder, he continued to live a normal life as a married man until his divorce in 1999. We have not uncovered any connections between Lowther and Mary Gregson, even though it was originally considered a possibility that Mary had known her killer.

'But we can draw a line under the case now. There's no doubt about whether he did it. Lowther stood there in court and admitted he was the killer.'

The psychological profile, said criminal psychologist Paul Smith, was wide of the mark. The fact that Lowther had remained married meant that he was trying to live as normal a life as possible and had been battling his slide into a reclusive life.

He said, 'The typical recluse in this situation would live with their mother or father or on their own. They don't normally live with a partner. And the fact that his marriage was before the murder was also very interesting. Very often, men who murder women cannot form proper relationships with them, but his marriage would seem to suggest that he could.

'What we do not know is what went on behind closed doors and it would also be interesting to find out why he separated from his wife. Living so close to the murder scene is bound to have had an effect on him. The only people who wouldn't be affected are the real cold-blooded killers and, fortunately, there are very few of them around, and his marriage suggests that he has some feelings.'

When the police had called round to his home with the buccal swab, and asked him to run it on the inside of his cheek, Lowther knew what would happen. But he gave the swab willingly, and said it was a relief when the police finally returned to arrest him.

DCS Taylor said, 'Here was a man who had never ever come to the notice of the police. So there was nothing about him that would distinguish him as a suspect at all. He was anonymous. He blended into the background. Nobody noticed Ian Lowther. At his former employment, he was so well liked that he was known as Uncle Ian. And if anyone had any problems with anything, or they wanted help or a bit of advice, they'd go and see Uncle Ian.

'To say it was a personal quest of mine to catch the killer would be too strong, but something like Mary Gregson is always there. It never goes away. The Mary Gregson case emphasises the importance of preserving the integrity of the murder papers themselves. It highlights the need to revisit and review homicide investigations in the light of scientific advances.'

Jailing Lowther to life imprisonment, Judge Michael Mettyear told him, 'Twenty-three years ago, you robbed an innocent woman of her life. You robbed parents of a child, a husband of a wife and a son of his mother. You took one life but ruined many others. Tragically, some of them have not survived to see you brought to justice. It was a wicked and brutal murder, accompanied by an indecent assault. All this loss and tragedy to satisfy a few minutes' lust. Thank goodness for the advances in DNA profiling; thank goodness for the determination of the police; thank goodness that the arm of the law is long.'

Finally, he praised the police for returning to the case time and again to look for a solution. He said the forensic scientists had done 'wonderful work' in producing the new techniques – and that those initially responsible for developing DNA profiling had probably never received the full recognition they truly deserved.

PC Eddie Gorny said of the murder, 'The whole thing was shocking for me and left a very great impression. I almost felt I was personally involved because I lived in Saltaire and my mum worked at Salts Mill. I always hoped there would be some way of cracking this case, but it seemed to me a very daunting task as time went on.

'When I was a young policeman, we'd never heard of DNA – the only testing was blood groups. It never occurred to me that you would be able to identify a person from their saliva.'

After Lowther confessed, PC Gorny said, 'I just felt

relieved. It was a great achievement which showed the public that we never give up and I felt very proud to be in the West Yorkshire Police Force.'

2

AN IMPERFECT MURDER

Norman Rae could not believe his luck. A man had telephoned a colleague claiming to have found the body of a strangled woman and wondered if his newspaper would like to negotiate exclusive rights to the story.

It was every journalist's dream, thought Rae. To have a story of such magnitude fall into his lap without any effort on his part seemed just too good to be true. Of course, his experience as a journalist – Chief Crime Reporter for *News of the World* – demanded caution at this stage. It might, after all, be a hoax and Norman Rae could find himself wasting valuable time on a wild goose chase, but he trusted his colleague's instinct about the story, which made him think that it could be genuine.

A few hours earlier on 8 August 1951, the man had telephoned the Nottingham area representative for the newspaper and casually enquired as to how much they might be willing to pay for his story. He had identified himself as one Herbert Leonard Mills.

At 12.30am that same night, Mills had been transferred to William Blackley, another reporter for the same newspaper. Intrigued, Blackley reached for a pad as Mills explained how he had found the body of a strangled woman and that no one else had been told – not even the police. Blackley tried to engage Mills in further discussion by enquiring as to where the body had been found, but Mills had a more urgent enquiry of his own, stating bluntly, 'I want £250 for the exclusive rights to my story.'

Unable to give him the commitment that Mills sought, Blackley suggested he put him through to one of his colleagues who might be able to assist and asked if he would hold the line while he located him. Norman Rae quickly made contact and took over, asking Mills to repeat the details for him so he could see if the story was likely to be of interest to the newspaper. Of course, he already knew it was of great interest, but he needed to play for time, while Blackley placed a call to Nottingham CID to report the potential murder.

Rae had engaged Mills sufficiently when another voice on the line interrupted and said that the caller's time was up. It was the perfect opportunity to discover the location. In his desire to progress the negotiations, Mills asked if Rae could phone him back as he had no further funds at his disposal. 'No problem, where are you?' asked Rae as casually as he could.

'I'm in Nottingham on 633191.'

'I'll phone you right back.'

Blackley passed the number to the police as Rae kept Mills chatting away.

It is fair to say that, at this stage, Blackley and Rae acted properly and that neither had any reason to doubt the caller's intention to make money from a chance find. However, both men had mixed feelings. On the one hand, it was a journalist's dream to have access to this type of scoop; on the other, someone was dead, presumed murdered, and this man was trying to profit from this information in a most macabre fashion. Worse still, he was trying to clinch the deal even before telling the police. But Rae knew it was a potential front-page scoop, and so immediately set off for Nottingham, telling Blackley he would call him later.

Acting on the tip-off from the *News of the World*, two detectives made their way to the telephone box that matched the caller's number. On arrival, they found the young man still in avid discussion with the newspaperman. Pulling open the door, they introduced themselves as police officers and removed the receiver from his hands. At the other end, Blackley heard the police officer speaking before the receiver was replaced and the phone went dead.

The detectives questioned the man.

'What is your name?'

'Herbert Mills.'

'We understand you know the location of a murdered woman.'

'Yes, that's right – I was just talking to the *News of the World* to see what they would pay.'

Slightly unnerved by Mills's odd priorities, they suggested that he should take them to the location of the body so they could see for themselves. He directed them to an area of Sherwood Vale about half-a-mile away – an overgrown orchard known locally as 'the jungle' – a remote spot frequented only by lovers.

It had been raining for several days and the long grass was sodden and soft underfoot as Mills led the men further into the undergrowth, before stopping and pointing to a dense patch of shrubbery.

Producing a string of beads from his pocket, he said, 'I found these just there on the rim.'

The officers lifted the lowest branch and peered into the gully to see a woman's body covered with a coat. The officers turned back to Mills.

'Where did you say you found the beads?'

'Just there on the grass near the shrubs.'

The beads were still fastened by a clasp.

'Are they just as you found them?'

'Yes. I know better than to tamper with evidence.'

'And when did you find the body?'

'Yesterday at twelve o'clock.'

Once again, the officers felt a surge of annoyance. Why had he left it so long before informing someone?

'What were you doing in this area?'

'I'm a poet. I come to this area quite a bit to write. I was writing a sonnet the other day and was sitting in this area trying to finish it.'

'And that was when you found these beads?'

'Yes – just there. And when I picked them up that was when I discovered the body.'

More detectives arrived at the scene, accompanied by uniformed officers, and began to make a detailed inspection of the site. Mills looked on as the officers entered the shrubbery and peered into the waterlogged gully. The body lay partly hidden under a small brown overcoat, her legs in grey stockings protruding from a plum-coloured floral dress. Although the body was in a state of relatively advanced decomposition, with the face blackened and bloated, the officers could clearly see the marks where her assailant had struck repeated blows, presumably in an attempt to subdue his victim.

As this was clearly a murder, the officers informed the head of Nottingham CID, DS Percy Ellington. While awaiting Ellington's arrival, Blakely continued to question Mills, who was by now looking more agitated.

Herbert Mills explained that he lived with his grandparents in Sherwood, some two miles from the crime scene. He liked to read and write poetry and often came to the area because it was so quiet and desolate. He had been there so many times he knew every inch of it. He had been trying to finish writing a sonnet and walked up there to help himself think and it was then that he noticed the beads when he sat down near the gully.

The officers listened to his story with interest and were not particularly inclined to disbelieve him. When they asked for his occupation, he replied that until a couple of weeks ago he had been employed as a bank clerk. Since his job had ended, he now spent his time on his two hobbies – poetry and crime stories. To earn a bit of extra money, he also backed horses and had enjoyed some modest success.

On arrival at the scene, DS Ellington took over the questioning and Mills accompanied officers back to the police station to complete a statement.

With the crime scene cordoned off, the officers began a more detailed examination. A partially filled snuffbox was found in the pocket of the coat draped over the body and a small distance away detectives found what appeared to be the victim's handbag. On examination, there was found to be a small amount of money, some ration cards and an assortment of papers, one of which was addressed to a Mabel Tattershaw of Longmead Drive, Sherwood.

One of the officers present at the scene recalled that a Missing Persons report had been submitted the previous Friday for that name and address. He immediately produced the report, which he had brought with him to the crime scene.

Ms Tattershaw was 48 years of age and descriptions of her clothing on the evening she had left home matched those of the dead woman exactly.

Back at the station, Mills repeated the circumstances of how he had stumbled upon the woman's body. He had sat down to conclude the wording of a sonnet that he had been writing, when he noticed the beads. When he leaned over to pick them up, he noticed something white in the undergrowth and upon closer inspection found it to be a woman's body.

Asked why he had not notified the police immediately, he stated he was worried and did not want to involve himself in the situation. He had subsequently walked away from the location and sat down to think things through, and realised that he was already involved because he had found the body. It was then that he had decided that, if he was to be involved in the situation, why not try and make some profit from it? He had chosen to phone the *News of the World* as this newspaper boasted the highest circulation and would therefore be more likely to offer the highest sum of money for his story. When the officers had arrived, he had been trying to conclude a deal with a Mr Rae.

The time delays incurred by Mills had annoyed the police but no one had any reason to suspect that Mills's version of events was anything but true. He did not know the victim and no possible motive could be established. However, the police asked Mills if he could provide them with samples of his hair and fingernail scrapings, which he gave voluntarily. This was, after all, just standard police procedure.

The young man was allowed to leave the police station as police began their enquiries. They needed to find out more about Mabel Tattershaw, including her social circle and her movements on the evening of her disappearance and death. They were happy to believe that Mills had not made the acquaintance of Mabel Tattershaw prior to discovering her body. The difference between their ages made any romantic involvement between the two most unlikely. The dreamy-eyed poet and the murder victim were an unlikely couple.

Mabel Tattershaw lived in a modest home in Longmead Drive with the younger of her two teenage daughters. She had little income and had taken in two lodgers to help with the upkeep of the house. It was one of the two lodgers who told of Mabel's departure from the house on the evening of her death.

'She was quite careful about her make-up,' the woman told police. 'It was almost the first time I've seen her wear any. You see, until a short time ago, Mabel lived a very simple life. She never went out, except to go to the cinema with her daughter or myself. On Friday, at about five o'clock, she dressed, made herself up and left, singing a little song to herself as she left.'

DS Ellington enquired further as to what was meant by 'never went out'.

The lodger explained that, until recently, Mabel had never had much of a social life, save cinema trips. She was usually back by 11.00pm, but now she would leave again after returning home. She hinted that she had met a man with a car. She told the detective of at least four men that Mabel had met in recent weeks, although she thought that all but one of them were fanciful flights of imagination.

The night before her disappearance, Mabel had gone to the cinema with a friend and had got into conversation for a time with a man seated next to her.

'But I've no idea what they talked about,' said the friend. 'And since it was very dark where we were sitting, I did not see what the man looked like.'

Meanwhile, police had been searching the crime scene for a possible murder weapon after the pathologist stated that he thought the victim had been bludgeoned with a heavy, blunt instrument. However, until a full autopsy could be carried out, the pathologist could not tell how long Mabel Tattershaw had been dead. It could be as recent as 48 hours or as long as six days.

Mills had been released from police questioning at about the same time that Norman Rae was arriving from London to cover the story for the *News of the World*. Mills, too, was keen to get together with Rae, as he still wanted to sell his exclusive and collect his reward, so they arranged to meet.

On the evening of 9 August, Rae booked himself into the Black Boy Hotel in Nottingham and suggested they both return to London the following day. The reporter offered Mills the chance to pen his own version of events for which the paper would be prepared to pay £80. Mills accepted the offer and looked forward to writing his own piece.

The following day the pair returned to London where Mills wrote his article, which appeared in the newspaper under the headline 'I SAW SOMETHING WHITE', which referred to his finding of the body. A photograph of Herbert Mills was pictured alongside his article, which gave him credit as the writer.

In the article, Mills recounted how he would sooner read or write poetry in some quiet spot rather than mix with a crowd. He stated, 'I like Shelley, Burns, Tennyson and Keats – books and beauty you might say – and I'm quite happy to be left alone with them. Yet – funny, isn't it – I like crime stories, too, and murders, if there's any preference. That's the irony of me running into a murder shortly after writing a sonnet.'

After describing his discovery of the string of beads, he wrote, 'As I straightened up, I saw something white below me in the fissure. It was the body of a woman. The white I had glimpsed was the left side of her face. Very white and pale it looked – seemingly dead. I was startled, wondering what I should do. I felt a little unnerved. I wanted to leave. On the way home, I sat on a bank to think. I sat there and read Shelley's *Ode to Death*. Then I thought of calling the newspaper.'

Mills returned to Nottingham on 11 August where he was largely forgotten by the police investigation, as they appeared to make investigative progress in other directions.

Police obviously considered it significant that Mabel Tattershaw had changed somewhat in the weeks leading up to her murder; from a sober, quiet woman who lived an ordered existence, leaving home at night only to go to the pictures, to a late-night reveller frequenting pubs on after-dark excursions. Detectives visited all of the pubs and taverns in the area in a bid to build up a picture of Mabel's life. No information was forthcoming from establishments in her immediate neighbourhood, so the police cast their net further afield.

One licensee they approached identified Mabel from a photograph and claimed she had been in her pub on the previous Saturday evening, some 24 hours *after* she left her home for the last time. The publican told police that a man, whom he described as 'rather pushy', had accompanied Mabel.

The man in question insisted on playing the piano and singing a few songs – passing his hat around in the process – which the licensee put a stop to. He was able to provide a fairly detailed description of the man. 'He was about 50 years old, with a fresh complexion, of medium height and well built. He had a scar under his right eye and walked with a limp. He was well-dressed in a black suit and trilby hat, with a blue tie and brown shoes and he sported a thin moustache.'

The publican continued, 'Like I said, he was a most aggressive chap, blustering at the lady all the time he was here.' The couple left the pub at around 10.00pm and the publican had seen neither of them since.

An acquaintance of Mabel Tattershaw was also able to confirm that her friend had been alive on the Sunday evening. The lady in question had been walking in a local park about half-a-mile from Longmead Drive when she saw Mabel walking with a man. From the description she provided of the man, it was evidently the same man who had been with Mabel in the pub. The police immediately launched a search for the man, hopeful for a speedy result, based on the man's pronounced limp, facial scar and the generally good description offered so far.

But the question remained – where had Mabel spent Friday and Saturday night, nights on which she had been seen in a park and a public house, the latter by someone who personally knew Mabel and was unlikely to have been mistaken? This was a piece in the jigsaw that police were eager to locate. She had obviously not spent the night at home even though her daughter had been living there and did not think fit to make contact on the Saturday either. This would be of particular interest if the report was accurate about Mabel walking casually through the local park on the Sunday evening some 48 hours after leaving home for the last time and some 36 hours after her disappearance was reported to the police.

Police made enquiries at all of the lodging houses and hotels in the area, yet none of their enquiries turned up a single clue as to where Mabel Tattershaw may have stayed on the evenings of Friday and Saturday.

As the investigation continued, the pathologist performed an autopsy at the Nottingham police laboratory. This involved an examination of the victim's clothes and a medical examination to establish cause of death, and perhaps retrieve any material left on the body by her killer.

On inspection of the victim's coat, the pathologist discovered three blond hairs of a man and they extracted several fibres, which had come from a blue cloth, which contained white thread in it.

A study of the victim's stomach revealed that, three hours prior to her death, she had eaten a meal consisting of potatoes, kidney beans, tomatoes and minced meat. From this information, the police were able to narrow down the time of death to the evening of 5 August, information that was released to the public. Frustratingly, this discovery meant that the two previous sightings of Mabel in both the park and the public house were apparently cases of mistaken identity, yet it had diverted much of the police's resources for a significant period of time. However, the forensic analysis had obviously made much progress in the investigation, saving the police from following up the reported sightings, which turned out to be false leads. Now it was official – Mabel Tattershaw had met her death on the evening of Friday, 5 August, three hours after finishing her last meal.

That Monday, an inquest was held by deputy coroner AG Rothera. The proceedings were uneventful, save for the public rebuke administered by the coroner to Herbert Mills for his delay in notifying the authorities.

Norman Rae attended the inquest and, following its conclusion, struck up a conversation with DS Ellington, who mentioned the bead necklace, which had caused Mills to look into the gully and find the dead woman.

'Did it strike you as strange, Mr Rae, that the clasp of the necklace was closed when Mills picked it up at the scene of the crime?'

'Very strange,' replied the journalist. 'I hardly know what to make of it.'

'It's also queer,' Ellington went on, 'that, while it was at first believed that Mrs Tattershaw had been bludgeoned to death from blows to the head, it turned out that she was, in fact, strangled. Yet when Mills first contacted you in London, did he not say that he had found the body of a "strangled woman"? How do you suppose he knew that, then?'

'I see what you mean,' said Rae, nodding thoughtfully.

'Moreover, when he wrote his story for your newspaper, he stated it was the white of her face that had caught his attention. Actually, her face was swollen and black from decomposition. What this all seems to add up to is that our Mr Mills knows considerably more about this whole affair than he has told us.'

Although the pathologist established the cause of death to be manual strangulation, not from the blows to the head, a man, probably wearing gloves, had initially possibly struck her about the head several times. These injuries had been superficial and had probably been dealt to lessen her resistance, so that the final act of killing could be carried out.

With a clearer picture of the murder, the police were still confused as to any reasonable motive. Mabel Tattershaw had lived a humdrum sort of existence and, as intimated by her lodgers, may have been prone to living in a fantasy world of sorts, creating lovers who simply did not exist. One lodger felt that the only real male friend she had established was the man with the car who she told her she had arranged to meet that Friday night. This date certainly sounded different to the others she claimed she had. On this evening, she had paid particular attention to her make-up, an act lacking on her previous sojourns, but which had not gone unnoticed by those who bade her a pleasant evening as she set off for what was to be her last night.

Meanwhile, Herbert Mills was attempting to obtain further funds from the *News of the World* newspaper. At

10.00am on 12 August, he contacted Norman Rae at the Black Boy Hotel and offered to provide more 'sensational information' for a sum exceeding £80. In retrospect, the information offered was to provide a turning point in the investigation in what had become something of a standstill for the police, when previous leads had all but dried up. Mills now suggested that he had, in fact, found the body on the evening of Friday, 5 August, not three days later as previously stated in a sworn police statement. With his suspicions aroused and armed with this new information, which was certain to cause a great deal of controversy, Rae refused to buy this information and told Mills that he would be informing the police without delay.

The journalist was now more confused than ever by this latest turn of events. The character and personality of Herbert Mills seemed unbalanced from what he knew of him. On one side, the quiet demeanour and soft brown eyes and overall sensitivity seemed in great contrast to the physical brutality meted out to poor Mabel Tattershaw and he found it difficult even to consider that this man had anything to do with her murder on that wet August evening. On the other side, however, was Mills's mercenary desire to benefit financially from his grisly find and to put his own financial gains ahead of contacting the police about the woman's death. And now he had made a complete turnaround in his original testimony saying that he had found Mabel Tattershaw on the evening of her death. Was Mills naïvely trying to extract more cash or was this new revelation true? If the latter was true, this would alter the whole focus of the investigation and Ellington's doubts about Mills's motives would be justified.

The police brought Mills in for questioning again, asking

him to explain the new details he had intimated to Rae. Although under pressure, he stated that he was only going to serve up the same information – but in a different format. It was, in short, a blatant attempt to obtain further profit. The interview with the police ran for 45 minutes and, when it was over, Mills contacted journalists from three rival newspapers, including a Mr Connolly from the *Daily Express*. He offered them more sensational information on the story – if they agreed to pay him.

At 10.00pm that evening, Mills met with Connolly and told the reporter how he had found the body on the Sunday evening and how he had covered her up with her coat as he thought that would be better. When Connolly advised Mills to contact the police, the latter replied, 'What about the money?'

The reporter claimed that it was contrary to sworn evidence provided by Mills and, as such, he could not use it. Instead, Connolly passed on the story to the police, but when they questioned the poet, he claimed that Connolly had attempted to persuade him to make the new bogus statement.

Based on these new revelations, Mr Porter, Assistant Chief Constable for Nottingham, and DS Ellington interviewed Mills at the police station. Mills denied that he had 'new and vital information' and said he was merely trying to resell his story to the press. His position, he said, had not changed since his original statement.

However, the detectives went on to question Mills about his description of the body. They considered that the man was describing Mabel Tattershaw either just prior to the murder or very shortly after.

The net was slowly closing in. Between 12 and 23 August,

pathologists found that the man's hairs on the victim's dress and coat could have come from Mills, having compared the sample he had voluntarily given with those found on the body. The wool fibres, too, could have come from the killer, as she struggled to fight off her attacker as he bludgeoned her with a heavy object and proceeded to strangle her.

Now, a whole new picture of the events of that Friday evening was beginning to emerge. He had previously stated to Norman Rae that the case would never get to court – and the perpetrator never apprehended. He seemed to be basing most of these assumptions on the lack of motive – something he felt was imperative in determining the likely suspects. He had acquired most of this knowledge from his interest in reading crime and murder stories. The use of forensic detection had evidently not yet entered the realms of crime fiction.

The police were growing more suspicious of Mills's version of events and Ellington, in particular, was convinced that the young man was heavily implicated in the murder. He decided to call Mills back for more questioning and would have done so had it not been for the intervention of the crime reporter. Rae suggested that Mills would clam up if questioned directly by the police and suggested that, as he himself had a rather trusting relationship with the man, he might be able to coax further details that would bring to light the true nature of Mills's involvement.

Ellington agreed, and so Rae arranged a further meeting with Mills.

'You're awfully clever,' Rae told him. 'You knew right off about the strangulation. It took the CID four days to discover how she had died.'

Mills said nothing.

'By the way, there is one thing that puzzles me. I should think the detectives would be curious about it, too. In your story, you wrote of seeing Mrs Tattershaw's pale white face, but it wasn't white at all when she was found because of its advanced state of decomposition.'

Mill's nervously chewed his lip. 'Look,' he said, 'I've not been telling the entire truth about this.'

Rae looked on expectantly.

'I'm afraid I should have done so at the start, but I was terribly afraid – after keeping quiet for so long. You see, it wasn't on Wednesday that I first saw her. It was on Sunday. Her face was white then. And I could see the marks on her neck. I guessed she had been strangled.

Rae looked disappointed. 'But you should have told this to the police. You still must.'

'No!' Mills snapped. 'I can't. And, if you mention it to them, I shall deny I ever said such a thing to you.'

'All right.' Rae shrugged. 'Have it your way, but you're making a mistake.'

When Ellington learned of this admission, he became fully convinced that Mills was the killer. Although he could show no motive or, indeed, opportunity to commit the murder, they were nonetheless pleased that Mills seemed to be cracking under the constant rechecking and questioning of his version of the events.

The senior detective suggested that, if they played their cards right, they may be able to crack the case completely. Rae was told to release details to Mills indicating that the police had gleaned further information that would soon lead them to the killer. Rae told Mills that they knew the man who had spoken to Mrs Tattershaw at the cinema, knowing full well the additional strain that this would place on Mills.

Mills took the report calmly enough. 'If the CID does turn up some chap who spoke to that woman in the cinema,' he said, 'what will it prove?'

'That would depend,' Rae responded. 'Perhaps nothing if the fellow isn't otherwise involved in the case. But if he should turn out to be someone already involved in the investigation, well ...'

'I see,' said Mills. 'But mark my words, they'll never be able to show definitely just who sat in the seat next to Mrs Tattershaw, even if they do find some possible suspect who was there that night.'

'I rather expect,' Rae continued, 'that the police will have other evidence in due course. Indeed, I would not be surprised if there are details that they have not yet released.'

Two days later, reports emerged in the Nottingham newspapers regarding the blond hairs found on Mrs Tattershaw's clothes and the woollen fibres under her fingernails. Police publicly stated that they were confident these clues would soon lead them to the identity of the killer.

The following day, Norman Rae received an urgent call from Mills summoning him back to the Black Boy Hotel in Nottingham. They conversed for a couple of hours about general topics such as betting on the horses, before more pointed discussions about conditions in prison and then, finally, about perfect crimes.

Suddenly, Mills blurted out, 'That was it. I tried to commit the perfect murder. I failed and want to get it off my chest.'

Rae nodded, barely able to conceal his triumph. 'I was certain that was why you asked me to come up.'

He handed Mills a pen and some hotel notepaper and told him to write down the facts in his own words.

Mills made a detailed confession about his murder of Mabel Tattershaw. He said that on the night of 2 August he found himself seated next to Mrs Tattershaw and another woman in the Roxy Cinema in Nottingham. He claimed that it was she who had endeavoured to make conversation with him and he had eventually responded, not wanting to appear impolite. She persisted with the conversation and he claimed to make it quite clear that he did not wish to continue. It was only when she insisted that they meet the following day that he accepted. Mills wrote that he had always considered attempting to commit the perfect crime and now here was the perfect opportunity to put his thoughts and plans into action.

The next day, on Friday, 3 August, Mills and Mrs Tattershaw walked out to the lonely orchard. She lay down on the grassy bank and it was then that he had noticed the beads around her neck and he asked if he could have a closer look. He looked at the beads, unfastened the clasp and placed the beads in his pocket. He had then seized Mrs Tattershaw by the throat and strangled her. He rolled her body into the gully and then left the area, reaching his grandparents' house at around 9.20pm.

Mills asserted that his confession was prompted by the growing threat that the police would finally get to him. The pressure had been steadily growing and he had read in the newspapers that the police had analysed hair samples that could be traced back to him. This had been the last straw and he had decided to confess.

Mills signed the confession then accompanied Rae to

the police station, where the two handed in the five-page confession.

Herbert Leonard Mills was charged with murder in late September 1951 and, after a preliminary hearing with the magistrates, he was sent to Crown Court for the trial.

Mills had noted in his confession that, if he had not reported the finding of the corpse, as there were no other factors connecting him with the case, he would have escaped justice. He had not known the victim, had no motive and, to that extent, he would have committed the perfect crime.

Although the idea of making money from reporting the crime earned him some cash and gave him the opportunity to write a 'crime story' for a national newspaper, illustrated with a photograph, the motive, as he himself had stated, was to commit the perfect crime. The authorities' initial lack of progress seemed to massage Mills's ego, but he insisted on involving himself in the investigation by changing his account, which led to further police suspicion and, ultimately, to his own downfall.

In the end, the crime was less than perfect and Mills's defence counsel was unable to persuade the jury that the murder was the act of an attention-seeking simpleton. The jury found Mills unanimously guilty and the judged passed a sentence of death.

On 11 December 1951, Herbert Leonard Mills met his date with the hangman at Winston Green Prison, and his brief moment of fame came to an abrupt end.

Poetic justice, one might say.

3

PSYCHO-TRAP

On 9 January 1986, Professor David Canter, behavioural psychologist, settled down in his seat for the 45-minute train journey from London to Guildford.

There was much occupying his mind. Apart from his normal duties as Senior Lecturer at Surrey University and his individual research interests, there was something else in his thoughts.

Two senior police officers had invited him to a meeting in London, just two months earlier. They wondered if it was possible that detectives could apply behavioural psychology to the challenges and difficulties they faced every day in the field of criminal detection and welcomed the academic's thoughts on the subject, giving him time to think it over and propose some ideas.

Professor Canter was considering this as he picked up

that day's issue of the *London Standard* and scanned it. Splashed across the front page was a feature devoted to the series of horrific sexual assaults, which had been committed in London over the past four years. Dubbed the 'Railway Rapists', the attacks were often the work of one rapist working alone, although in other cases there were two men, but always in the vicinity of London's vast railway network. The police evidently considered them to be connected, and the violence was worsening – the last attack had ended in murder.

Considering this to be as good a case as any to benefit from the proposed assistance, Professor Canter set about compiling a calendar of the crimes, setting them out in two columns – the first column for one rapist, the second for two, to see if he could find any obvious patterns to the attacks, which might show something about both individuals. Little did he know at that point that his assessing of the crimes was not only going to help the floundering police effort to catch these offenders, but also to introduce a new facility for fighting crime, which would highlight the case as a hallmark in the annals of British detection.

Once he had completed his train journey, Professor Canter worked further on the calendar of events until he was satisfied he had produced the best possible analysis. He sent it to one of the detectives who had originally met him, with the added note, 'Of course, the details I have are very sketchy, but I wondered if anybody had prepared a summary table like the one enclosed.'

What he had done, in fact, was to break down each crime into several sub-topics from all the gathered evidence. This included the victims' descriptions of their attackers – not only their physical appearance but their behaviour during each assault – and an assessment on the locations of the crime, thus revealing the *modus operandi* of the wanted men. He said he was curious to see if his notes made any sense to the police and whether his conclusions added anything to what the detectives already knew about the case.

Some months later, Professor Canter was invited to the Hendon Police College in North London to find that his ideas to divide the crimes into sub-groups – many details of which had now been entered on to a computer – had been drawn up by the detective team. Operation HART (an acronym for Harley's Area Rape Team), led by DCS Ian Harley, was now considering a second murder along with the first murder and multitude of rapes. The forensic evidence collected at the scene of each crime and the rather unusual reported behaviour by the attackers had led to the linking of the crimes.

Professor Canter said that it was this initiative that set in motion his personal journey to discover if a criminal's actions could systematically reveal his key identifying characteristics.

Other questions needed to be asked about the criminals. For example, did the assailant say anything to the victims before he attacked them? Were the victim's clothes pulled off, cut off or torn off? What sorts of threats were made to control the victim? Exactly what sort of sexual activity took place? How did he deal with her after the assault? Did he question his victim about her personal life, or about where she lived and, as did happen, was there an apparent self-disclosure about the assailant's ignorance of the locality of the attack? Did he demand that his victim acknowledge him as a person – that she kiss him, for example – which might imply that he was attempting to form some sort of intimate relationship with his victims?

Professor Canter related how profiling was a way of looking through the eyes of the offender. And so it was that he found himself in the incident room, sitting next to a detective constable who had been disseminating information from the psychologist's instructions. This particular analysis was the mapping of the crimes, down to locations and dates. A sheaf of transparent A4-sized maps were laid on top of one other, each sheet representing all the crimes committed within each year. When placed together, the sum total of the crimes could be seen, and, when all but one were lifted back, the crimes for only 1982 were evident. Professor Canter leaned forward to peer at that first spate of attacks, which were dotted in a small cluster in the North London area. He pointed to an area on the map and looked up at his colleague with a questioning smile. 'He lives there, doesn't he?' said the professor. The detective constable blinked and peered at the map.

Professor Canter said that the interpretation of the maps seemed obvious enough to him. He thought it highly likely that the first crimes committed in the North London area, either Kilburn or Cricklewood, indicated that the rapist, just starting out on his crime spree, would most likely attack in his own area. Following that, he would gradually seek out new pastures and spread his attacks further afield, as his confidence grew, and also in an attempt to further avoid detection.

The crimes had started way back in June 1982, when a woman was raped by two men near Hampstead station.

Over the next 12 months, the duo raped over 18 women, all within the five-mile radius of the pinpointed area of North London. The attacks ceased soon after that, and began again in 1984, but this time there was just one attacker. The first was at Barnes Common, then others followed in areas of West and North-West London, though police had no evidence to suggest that they were linked.

In July 1985, three women were attacked separately in one night in the Hendon and Hampstead areas. It wasn't until this point that police began to see the many similarities between the attacks and realised that they had a serial rapist on their hands.

Police had linked the crimes by identifying the unusual *modus operandi* of the rapist which remained consistent throughout the attacks. In almost every attack, the assailant began by 'chatting up' his intended victims – an unusual preliminary in sex attacks. The victim was then led at knifepoint to a lonely and isolated spot. Their hands were tied behind them in a 'praying' position, with a coarse type of string. Equally unusual was the way the attacker ended the attack by wiping the victim's private parts with paper tissues, and sometimes even used a small plastic comb and ran it through the victim's pubic hair, as if trying to minimise any forensic evidence.

Operation HART came into being, as DCS Ian Harley and his team of detectives began sifting through literally hundreds of known sex offenders. By the time they had a computerised list of the suspects, there were no fewer than 4,784 names. HART then began eliminating suspects, such as those who were currently in prison, or at least were in prison at the time of some of the attacks, and others for a variety of other reasons. Eventually, the list was narrowed down to 1,593. A month later, another possible suspect was added to the list.

That July, a man named John Francis Duffy attacked his estranged wife when he burst into her flat. Duffy used his expertise in karate to beat up the boyfriend of his ex-wife, who was so horrified at the violence that she reported him to the police. Duffy was arrested the next month and he became suspect number 1,594 in the HART inquiry.

In September 1985, another woman was raped in Copthall Park, near Barnet. A detective thought the description of the attacker matched that of Duffy and called him in for questioning. On 2 December 1985, Duffy was put on an identity parade but the victim, still suffering from the trauma of her ordeal, failed to identify her attacker.

Police had no choice but to release him and, less than a month later, events would take a turn for the worse, which would add a new urgency to the inquiry – a woman was murdered.

On 29 December 1985, 19-year-old secretary Alison Day left her home in Hornchurch, Essex, to travel by train to Hackney in East London to meet her boyfriend who worked in a local factory – but she never arrived. Her disappearance sparked a huge murder hunt.

She was found 17 days later as police divers searched the River Lea. Detectives later supposed that the killer had probably first spotted her as she changed from a main-line service at the busy junction station at Stratford, boarding a three-coach North London Line train to Hackney Wick. She began walking the remaining distance to the factory but never made it.

She was abducted at knifepoint and taken to some dingy lock-up garages, with her hands tied behind her back, and then raped. The attacker beat her unconscious with a brick, tore a strip from her tartan shirt and looped it around her neck. He then got a small piece of wood and inserted it through the slack material creating a tourniquet, which he gradually twisted tighter to kill her. Once she was dead, it was thought that the killer had carried her along the bank of the River Lea, filled her coat pockets with stones to make sure she would sink and threw her into the water.

Her body was discovered 9ft down on the bed of the murky waterway. The sheepskin jacket, still filled with stones, was discovered 200 yards further downstream.

DS Charlie Farquahar was put in charge of the investigation. He was determined to find Alison's killer; in fact, he had never failed to solve any of the 20 murder cases he had so far investigated.

A forensic report on the victim's clothes was prepared. Although her underwear was missing, the lab discovered foreign fibres – obviously from her killer – on the sheepskin jacket, jeans, shirt and on her body. Farquahar liaised with the HART team and quickly concluded that the similarities meant that the notorious rapist had now claimed his first murder victim.

It wasn't until 17 April 1986 that the killer committed his second murder. Fifteen-year-old Dutch schoolgirl, Maartje Tamboezer, lived in the village of East Horsley, near Guildford, Surrey, with her family. She had set out on her bicycle to ride to a sweet shop in the next village, West Horsley, via a path close to East Horsley train station. She had used this route as a short-cut to avoid heavy traffic on the busy A246 between Guildford and Leatherhead.

When she failed to return home, the alarm went up. Her bicycle was found quite soon after, abandoned in a wood near the path. Her body was close by and the same hallmarks were there. Her hands had been tied from behind, her thumbs pointing up in the 'praying' position. One of her socks had been stuffed in her mouth. She had been tied up, raped, viciously beaten, then strangled with the familiar improvised tourniquet – also known as a 'Spanish windlass' – which had also been used to strangle Alison Day, this time using the victim's scarf as the ligature. It was this murder which sparked the biggest manhunt in the history of Surrey, and the HART inquiry became the biggest national murder hunt since the Yorkshire Ripper inquiry.

It was clear that the killer was playing soldiers – lying in wait, then ambushing his victims. As in the previous murder, her killer had attempted to destroy forensic evidence by pushing tissues into the victim's body before setting them alight. Forensics, however, did recover two pieces of evidence – a sample of the killer's semen was retrieved and stored away for future analysis, and an unusually small man's footprint was found at the scene of the crime.

On the path nearby, detectives discovered a length of heavy-duty nylon cord stretched between bushes at chest height, which either knocked her off her bike or merely barred her way, forcing her to climb off her bike and walk around it.

The most promising lead came from a railway guard on the 6.07pm train from Horsley to London. He recalled a small man wearing a blue parka jacket who rushed on to the platform just as the train was about to pull away from the station. The guard reopened the automatic doors to allow the man on to the train, after the man had collided with two women at the station.

A young woman passenger on the same train also reported how a small man of the same description – with staring eyes – had gazed at her fixedly several times before she got off the train at Bookham. These reports prompted the police to check thousands of train tickets for a copy of the man's fingerprints, but he had slipped through the net once again.

Even though both victims were murdered 50 miles apart, DCS John Hurst of Surrey CID only took a few hours to decide that both women had been victims of the same man. He called for a meeting with DS Farquahar and all were led by the head of Surrey CID, DCS Vincent McFadden.

Meanwhile, detectives identified the unusual coarse string that the killer used to bind his victims' hands. It was called Somyarn, a type discontinued in 1982 and sold to a few major customers, including British Rail. Detectives reasoned that that, if they found the owner of that particular ball of Somyarn, they would find the killer.

A forensic check on Maartje's clothes at the Home Office Laboratories at Aldermaston determined that the killer's blood was of a type known as Group 'A' Secretor. An advanced form of DNA testing, which involved measuring the blood enzyme called PGM, meant that the semen specimen would enable them to narrow down the odds much further. PGM testing breaks down people into ten distinct groups, and, in this case, the tests narrowed the field to an average of only one suspect in five.

Less than a month after Maartje's murder came another

one. Although the lady in question was only reported missing and was not found until July, detectives felt certain she had become the third victim. On 18 May, secretary Anne Lock went missing after getting off a commuter train in Hertfordshire. Anne had recently returned from honeymooning with her husband in the Seychelles, following her marriage a month before, and relatives could think of no reason why she should have gone missing.

She had left her office that day on London's South Bank, and caught a train to take her home to Brookman's Park, near Welwyn Garden City. She had ridden to the station on her bicycle and, when she did not return home at the expected time, her husband went looking for her, then called the police.

Two months later, Anne's badly decomposed body was found among the brambles near an overgrown railway embankment, not far from Potter's Bar golf course. Again, it had been set alight, and it took police just a few hours to establish that the killer had claimed his third victim.

Before this third victim was found, a new operation had been set up – Operation Trinity, so-called because it was a combination of the three police forces from London, Surrey and Hertfordshire, and all their computer records were merged with Operation HART.

It transpired from subsequent investigations that Anne had arrived at the station at 10.00pm, and made her way to the nearby shed where she had left her bicycle earlier that day on her way to work. When police checked the scene, they found that a bench had been hauled across the path like a barricade, which had blocked the victim's route – a very similar method to the one employed by the killer in the murder of Maartje Tamboezer, with her route blocked by the cord strung across the path at chest height between two trees. This was just one more example of a well-planned, military-type exercise.

It also transpired that, on Saturday, 17 May, the day before Anne Lock's disappearance, John Duffy had been arrested at North Weald railway station on suspicion of loitering. As with his previous arrest in Essex, he was found to be carrying a butterfly knife, but he claimed to use this for his martial arts classes at Kilburn where he lived. Duffy was released, but not before the Operation HART computer had logged his arrest.

Duffy was again brought in for questioning on 17 July, and was accompanied by his solicitor. He was asked to give a blood sample, but refused. At the time, detectives realised that the slightly built Irishman with the ginger hair and pock-marked face matched the descriptions of the rapist and killer. Particularly notable was his unique way of staring at people, and one description was forever repeated by victims – they talked of the assailant's cold, penetrating blue eyes which resembled twin lasers, as if piercing straight through them.

Even though it seemed that this killer had enjoyed a run of very good luck, he was spotted by some police officers days later in an area far away from the scene of previous attacks. He was walking along a lonely branch line at North Weald station, near Epping Forest, one of the furthest outposts of the Central Line Tube network. Both officers knew that Duffy was a prime suspect and they realised he could be reconnoitring the area for a future attack.

When they stopped and searched him, they found he

was carrying a butterfly knife, similar to the one described by some of his victims, along with a wad of tissues, which the killer used to eradicate forensic evidence. Duffy was taken in for questioning at Epping Police Station but, to the officers' frustration, it was thought that there was not enough direct evidence to charge him with anything.

Anne Lock's body was discovered in July 1986; again, her killer had suffocated her and tried to burn her body. Detectives sought a second interview with Duffy but found that he had been admitted to the Friern Psychiatric Hospital in Friern Barnet, apparently suffering from loss of memory. As it was discovered at a later date, he had persuaded a friend to punch him in the face and slash his chest with a razor, explaining that the police were trying to frame him for rape and murder. Then he staggered into West Hampstead Police Station saying he had been mugged and lost his memory as a result. Murder squad detectives were incredulous. He had been under observation and yet he claimed he had been mugged. Now he had escaped further surveillance by becoming a voluntary medical patient. When detectives sought to interview him, the medical staff refused on the grounds that they feared he might be distressed by the experience.

However, what the police did not realise was that Duffy was allowed to come and go as he pleased as he was only a part-time patient. When police overlooked this possibility, it led to another attack. On 21 October 1986, a 14-year-old schoolgirl was attacked and raped in Watford. But, for some reason, her attacker decided not to kill her. When detectives realised that Duffy was roaming free, he was put on round-the-clock surveillance. Within a few days, he was followed heading back to Copthill Park, possibly planning another attack. As this had been the scene of earlier rapes, it showed that he had obviously faked his claimed amnesia. The same month, Professor David Canter produced his psychological profile of the killer, which he passed on to the police.

DCS Vincent McFadden said, 'You can imagine the enormous police resources involved in undertaking the task of singling out many suspects and keeping them all under round-the-clock surveillance. The psychological profile proved to be a very useful management tool in terms of making a decision to concentrate police effort on one particular suspect.'

The profile was also important because the physical descriptions from the victims varied greatly, so it was difficult to produce a photofit.

The profile consisted of 17 characteristics, 13 of which proved to be accurate. Canter thought that the killer lived in Kilburn or Cricklewood, within three miles of the first few attacks in West Hampstead (Duffy lived in Kilburn); that the suspect was married but with no children (he was married but was unable to father children); that his marriage was in serious trouble (Duffy was separated from his wife); he was a loner with few friends (he had only two close male friends); that he was physically small and felt unattractive – a common profile for a sex offender – (he was 5ft 4in tall and had acne); that he was interested in martial arts or body-building to boost his physical appearance (he was a member of a martial arts club in Kilburn); he needed to dominate women (Duffy was a violent man who had attacked his wife – in fact, the only reason he became a suspect was because of this attack on his wife and he was therefore added to the computer database); that he fantasised about rape and enjoyed bondage (he often tied his wife up before sex); that he was fascinated with weapons, particularly knives and swords (he had a large collection of kung fu weapons at his home); that he fantasised about sex and violence with a collection of videos and magazines (Duffy had a collection of hardcore porn, violence and horror movies on video); that he kept souvenirs of his crimes (he was later found to have kept 33 door keys stolen from his victims and, after his arrest, his wife told police that Duffy claimed to have raped a young girl and he showed her a personal stereo which he had stolen from her); that he worked in a semi-skilled job as a plumber or carpenter, judging by the well-planned attacks, which involved little contact with the public (he was employed as a carpenter for British Rail, giving him a detailed knowledge of British Rail's south-east network, stretching from Northampton to Hampshire and to south-west Kent, taking in all of London in the process. He had gained detailed knowledge of thousands of miles of tracks served by hundreds of stations, which helped him work out the best locations for his attacks, such as understaffed, badly lit and secluded stations); that he was aged between 20 and 30 years of age (Duffy was 28 at the time of his arrest and had been a rapist for the last four years).

There were certain aspects of the offender's behaviour which intrigued Professor Canter, particularly chatting to the victims after the attack. Canter said, 'He could establish a relationship in a marriage, but over time his violent side would explode and ruin the relationship. He gave advice to some victims on how to get home, which showed he could be caring as well as violent. Often, men like this have had their relationships broken up completely by the time they turn to really violent crime. Among other things, they need to vent their anger and frustration out on someone else.

'At the core of rape is bizarre sexual activity. It is remarkably difficult for people to hide and mask certain aspects of their sexual behaviour which are indicative of the sort of person they are. There are a great variety of rapes. We look at how the attacker approaches the victim, what goes on in the attack, and what happens afterwards. From all the factors taken together, we try to build up an overall picture.'

On 11 November, Duffy was again placed on round-the-clock surveillance at his council flat in Kilburn. He was followed from the moment he left home to the moment he returned. When he realised he was being watched, he indulged the police in a cat-and-mouse game. He tried to give his shadows the slip by, on at least one occasion, jumping on to a train as the doors were closing. However, this was soon to end. On Sunday, 23 November 1986, senior detectives ordered Duffy's arrest and he was never released again.

On a search of his home, police found a number of knives, a video which showed people being murdered by strangulation and a copy of *The Anarchist's Cookbook*. This was an urban guerrilla manual, which listed ways to incapacitate people, silence them and even kill them. It stressed the importance of escape routes, and Duffy's knowledge of the railway network had certainly provided that.

Searching his mother's house, they found a large ball of the unique string, Somyarn, which was used to bind his victims' hands together. Back at his flat, police seized the entire contents of his wardrobe and sent it all away for microscopic analysis. A few weeks before the trial, detectives received news from the lab that 13 foreign fibres from Alison Day's clothes had been matched to those from a jumper owned by Duffy. Even when faced with this forensic evidence and the ball of twine, Duffy refused to answer any of the questions put to him. When it was announced in the press that the man charged with being the Railway Rapist had been arrested, Ross Mockeridge, Duffy's friend, who had helped him fake the mugging, came forward to inform the police that it had all been a sham.

John Francis Duffy was born in Northern Ireland on 29 November 1958, the second child of John and Philomena's three children. He was named John after the newly elected Pope John XXIII. Her mother was visiting relatives in Dundalk when her son was born.

While at junior school he joined the Catholic Choir as an altar boy. By the age of 12, he was a shy youngster but enjoyed swimming and judo at school and joined the Scouts and Army Cadets. A former classmate said of Duffy, 'He was useless with girls, useless at lessons, and totally uninterested in things like sport and music. No one liked him. He was short and spotty-faced, the sort no one could get on with. And he was always rubbing people up the wrong way.'

At school, he was considered academically weak but encouraged to seek a job where he could 'use his hands'. In April 1975, he enrolled on a City & Guilds craft certificate at a firm in Camden as an apprentice carpenter, training in carpentry and joinery. His work was considered poor and he was not offered a job at the end of the apprenticeship. He was a well-known company absentee who seemed to be off work more days than he was present.

One of his workmates said, 'I knew him well, but I knew his family better. They were God-fearing, decent people, who believed in decent values, which is more than I can say of him. He just wouldn't stick at his job. His mind always seemed to be anywhere except on the job in hand.'

Years after his arrest, he was still remembered for his staring eyes, which his victims would mention to police time and time again. When he wasn't at work, he would frequent the Queensway ice-rink in Bayswater. His favourite trick was to annoy the other skaters by deliberately colliding with them. When they fell to the ground, he would roar with laughter at the spectacle.

For the next two years, he worked at a building firm before landing a job with British Rail in 1980. He was based at the Vehicle and Furniture Department at Euston Station. His work there was rated as poor, and was considered by colleagues as solitary and aggressive – on one occasion, he had to be restrained from attacking a colleague.

Duffy married Margaret Byrne in June 1980 at Camden Register Office. Although her parents took an instant dislike to him, she saw the best in him and they married in a secret ceremony. However, when the couple were unable to produce a child, Duffy blamed his wife, although it turned out that he had a low sperm count and it was therefore not Margaret's problem. This is about the time that Duffy became interested in fantasies of sexual violence and bondage.

The couple separated in 1982 and this is when the attacks

began. Several times, they tried to repair their marriage, including once in 1983, and soon after this Duffy resigned from British Rail. During that trial reconciliation, Margaret would go out to work and do overtime to support them while Duffy stayed at home and watched his horror and kung fu videos. They split permanently in March 1985.

There were certain criticisms levelled at the police during the investigation. The hunt for Anne Lock had lasted six weeks after her disappearance and yet she was discovered three weeks after the search had been called off. The police had already searched the thick undergrowth on the railway embankment where her body was eventually found by a team of railway maintenance workers, which was not situated that far from the railway tracks. By the time her body was discovered, it was already in an advanced state of decomposition and yielded few forensic clues.

Another error occurred when a Mrs Susan Donaghue reported to the police her chilling encounter with a man fitting Duffy's description – whom she described as 'a man with staring eyes'. The man had followed her on to a train between West Hampstead and Homerton on the North London Line – a long journey covering 11 stops. The man had continued to stare steadily at her throughout the journey, to the point where she became so frightened that she fled from the train, pushing her way through the crowds of startled commuters. Mrs Donaghue didn't immediately report her experience to the police but, after she did so, she heard later that no action had been taken. She reported her experience to two London police stations, offering her help in identifying the Railway Rapist, but the messages had never been passed on.

And yet Mrs Donaghue's encounter happened just a few days before Duffy killed Alison Day in the very same area.

At the time of Operation HART, there were criticisms that the system had become too bogged down in the multitude of computer checks when officers could have been out interviewing suspects. However, senior detectives rejected the critics pointing to the operation's vital sifting and analysis of evidence which was essential when applying Professor Canter's profile to the list of suspects. Not only did it lead to Duffy's arrest, but the computer records also culminated in the arrest of two other rapists who were guilty of attacks in similar areas.

Despite the criticisms, DCS Vincent McFadden of Surrey CID said, 'I am quite satisfied that everything was done as quickly as possible to bring this man to justice.' He rejected suggestions that officers had been slow in tracking down Duffy.

'A very professional job has been done,' he said. 'The right man was put into the system. It was picked through and it was shaken until he came out. I would attack the credibility of anyone who said there was a little bright reflective arrow pointing in his direction.

'More than 100 police officers were involved at one time in the search for Duffy. The profile proved invaluable in helping us to make a decision to put surveillance on one man. Putting a surveillance team on someone is a very manpower-intensive operation. Those officers could have been interviewing other suspects at that time, so it was crucial that we targeted the right man to justify those resources. You have to consider that there were other people on that list of 1,999 suspects, who were damned good suspects – some had been convicted of rapes near railway lines. Duffy had only domestic violence on his record when we arrested him.'

At his trial, Duffy was charged with two murders and five rapes. The body of Anne Lock yielded very little forensic evidence and the judge directed the jury to acquit him of her murder. Also, many rape victims refused to come forward and recount the attacks in court.

Duffy sat in silence and showed no emotion as he listened to the women and girls testifying against him about the rapes and sexual attacks he had inflicted upon them.

Mr Anthony Hooper QC, for the prosecution, described Duffy as a shrewd, calculating rapist who planned carefully and knew exactly what he was doing. 'He has a stare ... he drills with his eyes like two laser beams.'

On 26 February 1988, Mr Justice Farquaharson sentenced the killer to 30 years' imprisonment, telling Duffy, 'The wickedness and beastliness you inflicted on young girls hardly bears description. You are little more than a predatory animal. You behaved in a degraded and disgusting manner. On each of the seven charges you will receive a life sentence.'

After the trial, DCS Farquahar said, 'There is no doubt in my mind or the minds of all of the detectives on this case that Duffy did kill Anne Lock.

'There was one other extraordinary thing. If there was one thing his victims remembered about the man who attacked them, it was the description of his eyes. The first time I saw him, I knew he had to be the one. He really did have the most cold, penetrating, "laser-like" stare I had ever seen. He was without doubt one of the most evil characters in the history of British justice. Duffy is a walking advertisement for the return of the death penalty.'

Hurst said, 'I went to see Duffy after the trial and found that he was quite happy to do 30 years, because he wanted to shut himself off from the rest of the world. He did not show the slightest remorse for what he had done. He loved all the attention he was getting. It was just a big ego trip for him. The man is just a cold, calculating killer, and enjoyed what he did. He was the most evil man I've ever met.'

As Professor Canter says in his book *Criminal Shadows*, 'Through their actions, criminals reveal more than just what they are familiar with; they tell us about other aspects of their lives. We have to learn how to listen.'

After Duffy's conviction, the police's attention turned to Duffy's accomplice whom the killer refused to discuss. The press assumed that Duffy had dumped his partner in crime, that he had taken fright and was no longer willing to accompany Duffy by preying on lone women. Descriptions varied, and most attacks happened after dark, but the general description given was that he stood five or six inches taller than Duffy, was about the same age and had dark hair, a tanned face and wore a gold earring. Police always insisted that they knew who he was. Duffy only had two close male friends, but police dared not arrest their suspect as they had no evidence with which to charge him.

At one stage, they did target a suspect. They questioned him three times, and on one occasion the questioning lasted for six hours. When they made him take part in an identity parade, they could not find eight other men with a gold earring, and the witness did not pick him out. At the end of it all, they had no real evidence and had no choice but to release him. The man told the newspapers,

'The police had no evidence. They picked me up only because I was known to be John's friend.'

A curious postscript to the mystery was created by John Duffy himself who, after spending ten years in prison, had been persuaded by a prison psychologist to name his accomplice in crime. Duffy admitted to the court that he knew he would never be released and that his life sentences meant natural life sentences, but he wanted to 'clear his conscience' by naming the second attacker as David Mulcahy, with whom he had worked at Westminster Council in 1983, where Duffy was employed as a carpenter and Mulcahy as a plasterer.

Mulcahy, who was subsequently arrested, was charged with three murders, seven rapes and five counts of conspiracy to rape.

However, according to the killer, Duffy was the accomplice, apparently playing second fiddle to his partner in crime, and he willingly detailed the catalogue of attacks by both men. In March 1999, he pleaded guilty to further offences committed between 1975 and 1986, including the rape of Anne Lock.

Counsel for the Prosecution, Mr Mark Dennis, asked Duffy about the offences.

'Did you carry out all those offences on your own or with another on occasions?'

Duffy replied, 'With another on occasions.'

'Who was that person?'

'It was David Mulcahy.'

'The three women who were killed. Were you alone in relation to those attacks?'

'No. I was with Mr Mulcahy.'

Duffy recalled that the pair had met at the age of 11 on

their first day at Haverstock Secondary School in the Chalk Farm area of North London and they became very good friends. They used to look out for each other as they were both victims of bullies and both became interested in martial arts through watching films and vowing revenge after being bullied. They played truant from school and sometimes shot at people with air rifles. 'Although we both married in our twenties,' said Duffy, 'it didn't affect our friendship at all. I guess we never really grew up. I guess we went on doing the same things, like scaring people and lighting fires.'

Professor Canter's notion of where the rapists lived in relation to their crimes was accurate.

'We planned our attacks on women,' Duffy told the court. 'In the beginning, it was in areas that we knew well. We would plan it meticulously and we had balaclavas and knives. We used to call it hunting. We considered it a bit of a joke, a bit of a game. It added to the excitement. We would feed off each other's emotions. We never thought we would get caught. We were playing a game with the police and generally making it fun. We would put a tape on and sing along to it. A favourite which we played most times was Michael Jackson's *Thriller*.

'We attempted to do different accents to disguise our voices – Scots or Birmingham. It was mainly David. I wasn't very good at accents. With weapons, we sometimes used a replica gun, but we usually used knives. They do what they are told.' Duffy also claimed he was worried about Mulcahy's increased aggression and felt he had to intervene twice.

One of the pair's first victims described her ordeal from 1982, as she approached the office of a taxi company in

Kilburn, North London, in the early hours. When she saw two men in tracksuits jogging towards her, she thought nothing of it, until she realised they were wearing masks. They grabbed her and bundled her down a side road, sticking a large plaster over her mouth. One of them said, 'Don't worry, all we want is your teddy.' They pushed her over a wall into a garden and the taller of the two men put a knife to her throat. First, he pushed her to the ground and raped her, before asking if the shorter man was ready. He said he was and then he followed suit. The taller one – obviously Mulcahy – was the aggressor throughout the attack, who seemed to control not only his victim but also the shorter man, Duffy. She described Mulcahy as the horrible one and Duffy as the nice one.

Mark Dennis, for the prosecution, said that Mulcahy was the instigator and prime mover in both the murders and rapes. Unlike Duffy, he was the father of three children. He said Mulcahy and Duffy were joined by 'a unique and wicked bond' to rape, dominate and humiliate women. They went on what they called 'hunting expeditions' seeking lone women to rape near their homes.

Their second victim, a French restaurant manageress, was attacked in March 1983. She told the jury, 'I was fighting for my life.' Despite the attack, she continued to fight and bit one of her attackers on his hand, at which he snarled, 'You are dead! You are dead!' They dragged her along the ground before escaping when a car passed along nearby. The victim said both rapists were masked, looking like the IRA, with only their eyes visible.

Duffy broke down in court as he told of how his first victim begged for her life, before the pair mercilessly murdered her. The court had to adjourn after Duffy faltered and needed a break, while recounting how Mulcahy had begun strangling 19-year-old Alison Day. Duffy said of Mulcahy, 'He put some material around her neck and started twisting. '

Duffy told of how the attacks turned to murder after they changed their hunting ground to the North London Line in December 1985. Duffy threatened the victim with a knife, telling her to keep quiet, then took her to a canal and raped her, followed by Mulcahy. They took her to the far side of the canal to allow them time to escape back the way they had come. Duffy said that the victim fell into the canal, so he pulled her out but, when she tried to escape, Mulcahy became angry. Duffy faltered again as he recounted how Mulcahy strangled the victim with strips of material he had torn from her blouse in the unusual tourniquet fashion. Duffy said he was confused and scared, which is why he did not intervene, and Mulcahy said, 'We are in this together. Take it, twist it.' Duffy took hold of the material, half-twisted it and the girl dropped to the ground dead. Afterwards, Mulcahy weighed down her body with stones and threw her into the canal. Duffy described his accomplice as 'very excited, buzzing, saying it was the right thing to do. He was actually enjoying it, saying it gave him power – making the decision between life and death.' Mulcahy told him, 'It's almost God-like.'

A similar fate befell their second victim, 15-year-old Maartje Tamboezer, who was dragged across fields and raped. Mulcahy hit her on the head with a rock to knock her out then twisted the girl's belt around her neck. He told Duffy, 'It's your turn. I did the last one.' Duffy admitted he did not resist. 'I just twisted it until she died.' When Mulcahy attempted to burn the body, Duffy described him as 'excited, like a schoolboy'.

He claimed he was not present when their third victim, Anne Lock, was murdered. Duffy raped her, then Mulcahy sent him to get their car. When he returned with the vehicle, Mulcahy remained evasive saying that she would not identify them. Her body was found in undergrowth on a railway embankment two months later by railway maintenance workers.

The judge sentenced David Mulcahy to prison with a life sentence for each of the three murders and twenty-four years on each count of rape and conspiracy to rape. The trial had lasted five months and had been the result of a two-year investigation. After Duffy was told that he would never be released, he implicated Mulcahy in the attacks and the police spent two years investigating the confessions, many of which were verified by tracing victims of their rapes, who had spent 18 years trying to forget them, and also forensic evidence such as DNA profiling and advanced fingerprinting techniques. The judge, Michael Hyam, told Mulcahy, 'These were sadistic killings and, out of the two of you, I have no doubt it was you who derived gratification from the act of killing. These were acts of desolating wickedness. You descended to the depths of depravity.'

Regardless of the evidence stacked against him, his wife and mother of his three sons watched from the rear of the court gallery and still believed him to be innocent.

As Mulcahy was led from the courtroom, he looked across to his victims who had testified against him and smirked at them, but police knew that their job was not yet done. They had to look into hundreds of unsolved crimes, including murder and rape, to see if any could possibly be linked to the two killers.

Professor Canter told the authors that, as a psychologist, the case continues to fascinate him. He said, 'I keep on discovering further aspects of the Duffy case and its sequelae every few months.'

4

LIFE AFTER DEATH

It was an awful sight.

Jacqueline Poole lay on the living-room floor of her flat in Ruislip, North-West London, an electric cord wrapped tightly around her neck. She had clearly suffered a violent, frenzied attack.

She was discovered by PC Tony Batters on the morning of Sunday, 13 February 1983, after the father of Jacqueline's boyfriend phoned police to tell of his son's worry that Jacqueline had not been seen for several days and would not answer her door. A subsequent post-mortem revealed that the 25-year-old nightclub waitress had been strangled and sexually assaulted, with her jeans and knickers pulled down below her thighs, some time during the previous 48 hours.

Although many people were interviewed during the 15-month investigation, one Anthony James Ruark emerged as the prime suspect, but he denied going to the house or having sex with the victim and, although his alibi had gaps in it, there was not enough evidence to charge him. In the summer of 1984, the inquiry had not produced any new leads and the investigation was wound down. It was not closed, though – unsolved cases are never closed.

In 1998, when advances were made in forensic science, Mrs Poole's family urged DCI Norman McKinlay to reopen the case. He retrieved exhibits which had been saved from the murder scene, including clothes, carpet fibres and other items, and sent them off to the forensics lab, along with a sample of Ruark's DNA. There had been trace amounts of semen on the victim's clothes which had been analysed by previous, less-developed DNA tests, but the results were inconclusive.

One year later, DCI McKinlay got word from the lab. There was a match between the DNA sample from Ruark and the profile drawn up from the semen. However, the original sample from Ruark had all been used up from previous tests, so the result was gained in a most unusual way, by swabbing a microscopic slide on which the original sample had been tested. Microscopic pieces of Ruark's skin had been found under the victim's fingernails and his DNA profile drawn up from that evidence.

In the intervening years, he had married and had had children, having moved to Cirencester in Gloucestershire. When police were despatched to arrest him, he put up a struggle and attempted to escape.

At first, he declined to answer any questions, saying he had been in a pub with a girlfriend at the time of the murder. However, when confronted with the conclusive evidence, Ruark suddenly changed his story, saying that he had had sex with Mrs Poole on the night of the murder, but that she was still alive when he had left her flat.

Police then found that they had double the evidence. When the DNA profile was fed into the national DNA database, another match was found against Ruark. With no previous convictions, his profile had been taken by officers just three months previously when arrested for a minor theft.

Mr Nicholas Price QC, for the prosecution, told jurors that Mrs Poole could have been murdered by any one of her 41 previous lovers. The defence case was that, when Anthony Ruark left those premises, she was alive and well and in good spirits and so it seemed to follow that if, Anthony Ruark hadn't killed her, someone else must have gone into the premises after he'd left and finished the job. Mr Boyce said, 'I cannot bandy around allegations or point the finger of blame at someone and say you are responsible. But what I can do is say that Mrs Poole's reputation has been confirmed by the prosecution about the number of lovers, of various ages, who admitted having sex with her.'

Although Ruark had admitted to the court a string of previous convictions, ranging from vandalism to dishonesty, he denied murder.

Mr Price added, 'Despite his appalling list of crimes, there is not one conviction for assault or anything violent. Mr Ruark is saying, "Whatever my failings, I'm not a murderer."'

William Boyce QC, for the prosecution, told the jury that the clothes that Mrs Poole was wearing on the day of her murder had been submitted for forensic analysis two years ago. An advance in DNA profiling called Low Copy Number (LCN) had given police what they had been looking for – a DNA profile of her killer. He said, 'It showed Mr Ruark's body samples were on the deceased.'

Despite the police being deeply suspicious of his alibis, Anthony James Ruark, aged 40 at the time of the trial in August 2001, had been released in 1984, though the advances made in the 18 years since Mrs Poole's murder had unmasked him as the killer – and he was jailed for life at the Old Bailey.

The court heard that Jacqueline Poole had owned lots of jewellery – including several rings on each finger, worth a total of around £3,000 – which had been stolen by her killer and had never been recovered. Mr Boyce said, 'The defendant knew she had jewellery. He was her lover for a period. Although he was short of money before the killing, he was found to have more than might have been expected afterwards.'

Judge Kenneth Machin told Ruark, 'This was a brutal murder of a defenceless woman who had been nothing but kind to you.'

The judge praised police, particularly the head of the reopened inquiry, DCI McKinlay. 'But for his re-examination, this case, this matter, may not have come to trial.'

Senior forensic scientist Dr Jonathan Whitaker said, 'This case shows enormous benefits to the criminal justice system of our new DNA technology, combined with the national DNA database. It also shows how useful this can be in old cases where leads have gone cold. With the application of a dose of science and innovation, the investigations can at last bear fruit. People may think they have got away with murder for decades, only for science and the law to finally catch up with them.'

The victim's brothers, Terry and Lee Hunt, had attended every day of the trial. Terry Hunt said, 'Ruark has had 18 years of freedom that he should not have had, but this is finally justice. I have no feelings towards Ruark whatsoever, but I have nothing but praise for the police. She was a loving sister and we will never forget her.'

DS Tony Lundy, who was in charge of the original investigation, flew to Britain from his home in Spain to attend the trial. Outside the court, he said, 'This case is always one that bugged me. It was a thorn in my side, really. The most infuriating thing was not being able to give the family the satisfaction of a conviction. Imagine what it was like for this murdered young woman's family who had to live for 18 years not knowing who killed their daughter or sister. Thank goodness for the advances in scientific DNA. Ruark was always the main suspect and, although after some 15 months we closed down the inquiry, he was noted as the person most likely to have murdered her.'

But why exactly was Anthony James Ruark singled out as the most likely suspect just days after the murder? There are certain aspects of this case which were not passed on to the jury; in fact, even with the revolutionary DNA advances, they may have failed to get Ruark convicted if they had introduced another side to the investigation, which was kept officially under wraps until the murderer was finally convicted.

It all began in the home of 22-year-old Christine Holohan, who lived in a council house just a few hundred yards from the victim.

Holohan said, 'I lived in the area and had read about the murder in the papers. Then, one night, I woke up to my find my bed shaking and the lights flickering. I thought, Oh my God! then looked up and saw this blonde woman staring at me, tearing at my sheets in panic. Instantly, I knew it was Jackie and she told me what had happened. Over the next few weeks, she kept coming. She couldn't rest until her killer was caught. I had to contact the police.

'You could see at first that they didn't believe me, but then they realised all the information I was giving about the crime was right. At one meeting, I went into a trance and let Jackie take over my body. When the police asked for the name of the killer, my hand wrote the word "Pokie". It meant nothing to me – but that was Ruark's nickname. Then Jackie relived the whole scene of the murder and showed me what happened. It was utterly terrifying, watching through her eyes as this man strangled her. I saw his hands go round her throat and pull the cord tight.

'Jackie kept on showing me freeze-frame pictures of the scene and all I could do was write it down, pass it on and hope they'd catch him.'

Tony Banters had been the first officer on the scene at Jackie's flat and admits that he was astonished by the medium's revelations.

Tony said, 'She described everything much as I found it. She knew the victim's position, some of her injuries and clothing. She even knew that, in the course of robbing Jackie, the killer had left two of her rings – they would not come off. In fact, some of Christine's information was unknown to anyone at the time – except the murderer and the victim. When we asked for information about the killer, Christine described him in great detail, his age and month of birth, height, skin and hair colouring, tattoos, the type of work he did and mentioned his criminal history. She said the victim knew the killer and warned that friends would provide him with an alibi – not thinking him capable of violence – all now proved right. And when her hand wrote the name "Pokie", it was absolutely spine-chilling. We had already interviewed Ruark, but at that moment I knew we had got our man.'

Christine, who now lives in Ireland, said, 'I haven't been the same since it all happened. I still do my psychic sessions but I never let anyone get as close as I did with Jackie. I could never go through that again. It still haunts me. But I'm pleased they finally got that man, Pokie. Now I'm going to put some flowers on Jackie's grave – and I know she will be in peace.'

During the 15-month-long investigation, PC Tony Batters was a member of the murder squad. Within only a few days of the crime, he and a detective constable were despatched to meet Christine who told police she had vital information concerning who murdered Mrs Poole. When the two officers arrived at her home, Miss Holohan explained exactly how she had come by the information, as she was rather reticent about explaining it over the phone.

She told them how she had been 'bothered by psychic experiences' since she was a youngster living in Ireland, and went on to explain in great detail how she had been contacted by the spirit of Mrs Poole.

Although there had been only very brief press reports about the case, the two men found that the young woman knew more about the case than most of the officers investigating it. Christine told them that she was repeatedly hearing the voice of the victim, who had introduced herself as 'Jackie Hunt'. This had been Mrs Poole's maiden name, which had not been publicised. She had been married to Malcolm Poole, who was serving a prison sentence at the time of the murder, but they had divorced some time ago.

As former PC Batters said in an article he wrote for the *Police Federation Magazine*, 'My colleague Andy and I were sceptical at first, but our attitude changed quickly. To describe her as well-briefed would be an understatement. My contemporaneous notes of that interview are still available for independent review.'

PC Batters had been the first officer at the scene, where he had remained for many hours, and Christine described the scene just as the officer had found it, including the exact position of the victim, the injuries sustained and an accurate description of the clothes she had been wearing.

In a series of self-induced trances, first at her home then at a late-night interview at the police station, she reconstructed the crime step by step, relaying the events of that evening as they unfolded. For example, police believed that the whole attack had begun in the living room, but it had actually started in the bathroom. Christine described a towel-rail which had been pulled from the wall and a rug which had been overturned during the struggle. These details had not been released to the press. The only people who could have known this were the victim, her killer and the detectives. Although most of the jewellery had been stolen by the killer, two of her rings were still on her fingers because the killer could not remove them. Again, this is another detail which was not released. Mr Batters relates that Christine recounted various trivial details, like the position of crockery in the kitchen and the fact that the cushions on the settee in the living room were untidy, and all were described as if she had been present. These could have been lucky guesses, he admits, but it is unlikely that information of such a trivial nature would have been passed on to her by someone else. Mr Batters does wonder if the trivial details had been related to lend credibility to the more significant issues. Although Christine had not known Jackie, she was able to say what she had been doing before her murder, and that Jackie was suffering from depression following her divorce, that she felt unwell and had just been given a prescription from her doctor, that she intended to be elsewhere on the night she died, and that two men called at her door prior to her death, on innocent business. How could Christine have faked these details?

There was information concerning names connected to the victim, some of which did not make sense until after the trial. Christine told how Jackie had constantly asked for 'Terry'. Although Jackie had been a member of a large family, it was her eldest brother Terry to whom she was closest. Also, 'Barbara Stone' was a name which the voice continually repeated. This meant nothing until after the trial, 18 years later, when Mr Batters discovered that it was the name of Jackie's friend who had been killed in a car accident over a year before Jackie had been murdered.

The only significant detail which Christine got wrong was the date of the murder. The pathologist concluded that she had been killed at around 9.00pm on Friday, 11 February 1983, two days before she was found, whereas Christine said it was Saturday night.

When asked for the killer's name and where her stolen jewellery was located, Christine told the officers that she could not understand Jackie's reply. She was repeatedly saying a word which made no sense to her whatsoever. She said it sounded like 'Porky' or 'Poker'. Christine told them, 'She keeps repeating a word. It's not clear and it doesn't sound like a name. She says she wants to write it down!' Christine reached for a pen and notebook, paused a while as she went into a trance and scribbled down two words among some illegible scribble. It read, 'Pokie' and 'garden'. Pokie was Ruark's nickname, and 'garden' seemed to indicate that the victim's jewellery had been buried in a garden. Says Christine, 'She kept saying garden when I asked about the jewellery.' Mr Batters said that, as a direct result of this, the gardens of Jackie Poole and Anthony Ruark were both dug up by police, and further investigations continued through interviewing and reinterviewing other witnesses about Ruark's movements on the night of the murder, but to no avail. There was no sign of the missing jewellery, and the matter has never been resolved.

Other words scribbled down included 'Ickenham', which was the name of the village which Ruark said he visited after he left the pub in Ruislip and then ran out of petrol there, though why this should have been relayed by the supposed spirit of the deceased woman has never been satisfactorily explained. Also, Ruark and his girlfriend had offered witness statements soon after the police's appeal for information, in which he said they were travelling by train at the time, giving them both an alibi at the estimated time of death. His claim that he was riding a motorbike was dismissed after it was revealed he was a disqualified driver.

Many of the press reports in the media have stated that,

when the suspects were so numerous, it was Christine's information which persuaded police to single out Ruark as the prime suspect in the case. Tony Batters says, 'Despite our particular interest in him and his dubious alibi, Ruark had at that time to be viewed in the context of a score of possible suspects, several with alibis which could not be corroborated. The officer leading the investigation, DS Tony Lundy, decided to treat the information offered by Christine Holohan in a very matter-of-fact way. He viewed her as nothing more than an intermediary who was relaying information, supplying information from witnesses who preferred to remain anonymous; information such as the name of the suspect, supported by details which could validate the source's credibility.

Mr Batters says that almost all of the hitherto unknown information offered by Christine did come to light during the investigation, but, without corroborating eyewitness statements or forensic evidence to back them up, they could not be offered as evidence because they could not be verified just after the murder.

He acknowledges that the police may have been victims of a set-up between Christine and some unnamed party, but it is considered rather unlikely. Mr Batters concludes, 'We were never to find the remotest connection between her and anyone who could have told her all that she seemed to know. In theory, and given enough time and resources, she could have collected much of her information through contact with the actual killer or someone in whom he confided, and with the victim's relatives and friends, and also with murder squad officers. I collated every statement through the 1983–84 investigation. However bizarre the conclusion, the only single source of all her knowledge had to be the victim. If any lesson is to be learned, it is that one should not dismiss the possibilities out of hand.'

Having been with her in that first interview for one-and-a-half hours, Mr Batters and his colleague 'tested' Christine by trying to get her to admit that she had been given some of this information by the victim's family or, perhaps, even by a member of the murder squad, although Christine insisted that she had only one source of information – the dead woman. In a bid to persuade them otherwise, she offered to give one of the two men personal details about their life that she could have no way of knowing. Mr Batter's colleague volunteered.

Christine asked for an object belonging to him and, when he gave her his car keys, she performed a psychometric reading of his life. The detective was quite amazed. One detail, too personal to be divulged, was absolutely correct; she also told him he had received a letter concerning 'essential electrical work' which needed to be done. His building society had written to him the previous day offering a mortgage on the condition that the house be rewired. The third point was that the detective would be transferred to another police division. Although extremely sceptical about this, within a few days, the detective was transferred to another division.

The medium's intervention in this case seemed conclusive, and it has since become regarded by paranormal researchers as one of the most convincing arguments of post-mortem communication – in other words, the dead communicating with the living.

Tony Youens, a researcher for ASKE (Association for Skeptical Inquiry), teamed up with Adrian Shaw, a police detective who had taken an interest in the case, and they wondered if there might be a non-paranormal explanation for the events as related by the medium. Mr Youens consulted with Mr Batters, comparing notes on the case and discussing the details, and found that they were both essentially agreed on the facts, though each came to a different conclusion.

Youens stated in his investigation report that, if it was possible to show that Christine Holohan could have provided the information without the use of mediumship and speaking to the deceased victim, it should be regarded as more likely. In the past, Youens has practised the art of 'cold reading', a method of coming up with personal details about someone without any prior knowledge of them and he has fooled people into believing he is psychically gifted. He has not done this to defraud anyone, but simply as a way of showing that at least some mediums are, in fact, conjurors, rather than acting as messengers between the living and the dead. Youens and Shaw investigated various aspects of the medium's claims and found that many aspects which had been regarded as outstanding insight into the murder do not actually stand up to close scrutiny. 'My initial thought,' said Youens, 'was that Holohan had had this information passed to her by someone who wanted to alert the police to the identity of Ruark and yet to remain anonymous.'

Much has been made of the medium's revelations of Ruark's pullover which was found in his dustbin and subsequently tested for forensic evidence. Did police search for this pullover as a direct result of the medium's information about its existence?

'It is argued,' says Youens, 'that, without the timely

recovery of this piece of clothing, Ruark may well have once more escaped justice.'

Youens looked at statements by SPR researcher Montague Keen who said, 'The fact is, without the help of the medium's statements, the police would not have retrieved the pullover or interviewed and taken statements from everyone with whom Ruark came into contact that evening. Nor, according to Tony Batters, would they have checked and verified all Ruark's movements during the previous fortnight. The pullover became vital as it was his only garment retained for forensics, and it showed numerous exchanges of blood and saliva from Jacqui Poole to him. This proved an act of violence, as opposed to the intimacy which he claimed in his defence at court.'

Says Youens, 'Just how significant did this piece of evidence turn out to be? When asked by Adrian Shaw, DCI McKinlay couldn't even remember the pullover. DS Tony Lundy does recall "fibres" being mentioned at the trial, but he and McKinlay are emphatic that the conviction was based on DNA taken from the killer's skin which was found under the victim's fingernails, and semen samples taken from the victim.

'In my first conversation with Lundy, he said Ruark was immediately suspected and held in custody within the first 24 hours of the investigation and it would have been during this time that Ruark's premises would have been searched and the "vital" pullover discovered (at this time, if a suspect was under arrest, no search warrant would be required). This would have been at least three days before Holohan was interviewed. The officer who brought Ruark in (but not actually under arrest) also thought this happened within the first 24 hours. However, according to Tony Batters, Ruark attended voluntarily on that first Monday. But, even if his being taken in wasn't until Tuesday, this was still two days before Holohan was interviewed. It would certainly have been possible for Holohan to obtain at least some information. Jacqui Poole would, no doubt, have been discussed in detail, as would Ruark.'

The crux of the whole matter is the medium's source of information. Could Christine Holohan's information have been a mixture of what she picked up from people discussing the details of Ruark and Mrs Poole, information gleaned from newspaper accounts, and sheer guesswork?

Tony Batters asserts that the 150 separate pieces of information could not have come from one single source other than the victim or the killer, but is this necessarily the case?

Youens argues that, at the time of the murder, both Ruark and Holohan were 22 years old and it seems likely that they would have mixed in the same social circles. It is certainly possible that Holohan could have come by much of the information she delivered through social contact with people who knew either victim or killer or both. He says, 'It is surely reasonable to assume that this murder is going to be the subject of intense local gossip, particularly in places like the local pub, The Windmill, which was not only the place from where Ruark had been taken in for questioning, but also where he regularly drank with his girlfriend, as indeed did Jacqui Poole and her boyfriend. The victim had a wide circle of friends and acquaintances, including a close friend who told the police of her rejection of Ruark's attempts to flirt with her, along with a great deal of personal information about Jacqui herself.'

Batters said, 'During the course of the investigation, we received several calls from people offering their services as psychics, but they talked nonsense. Christine was exceptional. We were never to find the remotest connection between her and anyone who could have told her all that she seemed to know.'

However, Adrian Shaw noticed that Holohan's way of relaying information kept switching for no apparent reason. He said, 'Sometimes, Holohan talks as if she is Jacqui Poole speaking directly through the medium, while at others she slips back into the third person as if she is merely repeating what Jacqui has told her.'

Among other statements, Holohan said, 'Two men called earlier. She didn't want to go.' According to Tony Batters, two people were due to take Jacqui to her new temporary job at Whispers nightclub and called for her at 7.45pm, but Jacqui did not want to go as she was feeing unwell. The father of Mrs Poole's boyfriend had called round to her flat about an hour prior to the murder. Did Jackie mention this to him? It is highly likely, as she was not feeling well, and this would have been mentioned. Did he then mention it to someone else? And then, either they mentioned it directly to Holohan, or to someone else when Holohan was present, or passed it on to her at a later date. Youens says that, 'It is impossible to know what sort of information was discussed publicly by the many friends and acquaintances of the victim, but people like to play amateur detective and aspects of the crime could have been discussed.'

The medium also made a number of ambiguous

statements. She told the police about Ruark, saying, 'You have got the right group,' rather than something specific like, 'You had the right man in custody last Monday.'

Holohan also described seemingly trivial detail – unconnected to the crime – which may have been used to convince the police that the medium could impart knowledge of the arrangement of objects in the flat because she had been told as such by the murder victim. One such example is the statement, 'Two cups in kitchen. One washed up. She made cup of coffee.'

Youens draws attention to this statement, saying, 'What might these words actually mean? How many ways could they be interpreted? Is she saying that Jacqui Poole only had two cups in her entire kitchen? One in a cupboard or work surface and the other washed up on the draining board? Did she make coffee for the murderer? Or a friend? Or perhaps it implies that she made a cup of coffee for herself. Tony Batters fits the facts to the remarks. If one cup, washed or unwashed, had been found, would Holohan's statement still fit? When one looks at the statement in this light, then the answer is an emphatic "yes". This was a trivial detail and did not relate to the crime. Even Tony Batters suggests that this could have been merely guesswork. If it had been wrong, it would have been difficult to disprove.'

Other information provided by Holohan regarded Ruark's criminal history, and she referred to an insurance fraud, which, Batters says, 'Ruark subsequently admitted to us. Christine told us we were to look for scratches, later attributed by him to a collision with a hedge. He would have had a social connection with the victim through a friend who was in prison, and had visited the address before to perform a task. Indeed, he had done – to check the fuse box which he was to switch off during the murder months afterwards. She warned that the killer's friends would support his alibi, and that none of them would believe he was capable of violence. Each of these facts applied to the man who has now been convicted.'

Batters said, 'Almost all that Christine said would have, and indeed did, come to light during the investigation, but we lacked all the vital evidence of witnesses and forensics. Even an appeal on *Crimewatch UK* failed to produce any useful leads. Hearsay evidence is not admissible in criminal proceedings, of course, even less so when it could come from the hereafter!'

However, concerning the pullover, Youens stated, 'I find it curious that Holohan gives a pretty detailed description of Ruark, but not once describes what he was wearing at the time. If this pullover was of such significance, why didn't she say what he was wearing, particularly after she described in detail what the victim had been wearing?'

Youens and Shaw have shown that many of the statements made by Holohan could have come from different sources. It has been emphasised that the detailed information about the stolen jewellery could never have been known to Holohan prior to her interview, and yet, following the murder, the local paper, the *Ruislip and Northwood Gazette*, ran a front-page story about the case, giving a detailed list of the jewellery taken from her flat.

Tony Batters stated that Holohan knew that, in the course of robbing Mrs Poole, the killer had left two of the many rings she wore, because he could not remove them from her fingers. However, the notes which Batters wrote at the time were based on what she actually said, so could they have been misinterpreted? Batters recorded the medium's following statement: 'Someone knows about the jewellery. She had some stolen. Some left. Was there another ring from these two?' But she doesn't actually say that two rings are left behind. As these notes are taken from a verbal statement, Youens suggests that the medium merely said, 'Was there another ring from these, too?' which was then misinterpreted by Batters as a 'psychic' insight from what is now merely reduced to a general statement.

It could be argued that, despite Lundy's claim that no action was taken in regard to what Holohan told police, he may have ordered the victim's respective gardens to be dug up in search of the stolen jewellery, but if so it did not result in further evidence. The jewellery was not found and all it achieved was to waste police time.

Regarding the personal information that Holohan gave to Tony Batters's colleague about his life, to prove that she really was in contact with the dead woman, Youens says that, if the information was of the type he thinks it was, he can see why the detective was impressed. As can be seen with other ambiguous statements, the interpretation of what she said may have been different from what she personally intended to say. He regards this information possibly as a simple case of 'cold reading' which he has practised before, quite successfully. 'As far as I know, there are no notes of what was actually said as opposed to what was remembered. What Tony Lundy is sure of,' says Youens, 'and he has stated this unequivocally, is that at no time during the investigation did he take any action based on information supplied by Holohan. He only ever followed normal police procedure.' This brings into question the statement that Ruark was only arrested because he was named by Holohan as being the killer.

In conclusion, Youens states, 'As far as I can tell with any certainty, she provided no information that affected, influenced or progressed the investigation in any way whatsoever. If you remove all the personal references to Jacqui Poole and Anthony Ruark, which I believe would have been easy to find out about at The Windmill and other local pubs, then the notes are reduced drastically. If all the other details had been removed, would the police have been so impressed with the information that was left? Personally, I doubt it.'

Whether or not Holohan's source of information came from the deceased victim, or a variety of sources with whom she came into contact, is pure conjecture, but the fact is that Ruark was eventually imprisoned. Tony Batters stated, 'I know Jackie's family are delighted with the help she [Holohan] gave, so there is a special thank you from them as well.'

On 24 August 2001, Ruark remained impassive as he was convicted of murder by a unanimous jury and sentenced to life imprisonment. DCI McKinlay stated, 'We hope Jackie and her family feel that justice has at last been done.'

5

ASHES TO ASHES

On 27 June 1999 it was a pleasant summer's day which gradually turned into a warm, clear evening. Mandy Power was out shopping with her daughters, Katie, aged ten, and Emily, aged eight. They had enjoyed a pleasant, late afternoon together and eventually decided to return home to their house in Craig-Cefn-Parc in the Swansea Valley.

They were in no particular rush and eventually arrived home to their rented, semi-detached house in the early evening. On arrival, they ate tea and the children played and watched some television. Mandy's invalid mother, Doris Dawson, was upstairs in bed as usual. Mandy had gone up with some tea and chatted for a while.

The children went upstairs and readied themselves for bed, while Mandy remained downstairs clearing up and preparing to relax for the evening. With everything out of the way and the children in bed, Mandy settled down in front of the television. A few hours passed until, quite unexpectedly, there was a knock at the door. It was late, after 11.30pm, but Mandy had taken visitors at this time before and so she answered the door. She recognised the person standing there and allowed them to come in. They spoke for a while, but she was not keen to prolong the conversation. It was at this point that a perfectly lovely day, and a perfectly normal evening, would turn into a monstrous bloodbath that would destroy three generations of the same family.

Mandy had gone upstairs to her bedroom, possibly to prepare for bed. The visitor had followed her upstairs; by now, a violent rage had built up inside him. As she turned to face him, he struck her with an almighty blow with a long pole, which knocked her to the ground. Although dazed and in pain, somehow she found the strength and presence of mind to scramble past her assailant and flee to her mother's bedroom. Doris Dawson was awake when her daughter came rushing in – a state that would ultimately spell the end for her as well. Doris would have recognised the assailant, now holding the pole above his head and raining more blows down on Mandy's lifeless, blood-spattered body.

Unable to move, she could only stare in horror and disbelief as her daughter was pummelled to death. By now, Doris may have guessed her own fate; she had witnessed the events in full, and so she would be next in line. Heavy blows were directed at the old lady and she, too, perished in her blood-soaked bed. Heading back on to the landing, the killer came across ten-year-old Katie, who walked straight into a series of heavy blows to the head that killed her. He knew there was another victim to deal with, and headed to the other bedroom, where he found Emily cowering in the corner. Her small, eight-year-old body was unable to withstand the ferocity of the attack that the visitor unleashed, and she too perished under several heavy blows, leaving her in a bloody heap on the floor.

The carnage had come to an end and now all was silent. The multiple killer stood still and took in the reality of what he had done. He let his weapon fall to the floor and began to pace the room slowly, his anger subsided, replaced by logical thought. Cool and calculating, he carefully considered his next move. He took stock of the bloodbath around him and decided that he must adopt a course of action that would diminish his chances of detection. But he would have to be very careful. He was not stupid; forensics would be crawling over this house the following day, searching every nook and cranny, probing every fibre of every carpet and curtain. He would have to be very, very careful. But how could he destroy all the evidence of what he had done?

The thought came to him in an instant – fire. He stalked his way from room to room, grabbing any suitable material and setting it alight. When everything was ablaze, the killer disappeared into the night, leaving one of the bloodiest scenes that South Wales Police had ever encountered, and one that would shortly turn a small community inside out, as the police sought to locate the monster who had wiped out a whole family.

The Swansea Fire Service received a call from a neighbour at 0427, in the early hours of 28 June, stating that a house on Kelvin Road, Clydach, was on fire and that it looked pretty much consumed. The tenders arrived only minutes later and found neighbours in the street, and the kitchen of the house engulfed in leaping flames and searing heat. The firefighters were overwhelmed and soon they had to retreat to the safety of the road, pressed back by the sheer scale of the blaze. Eventually, their powerful water jets brought the fire under control, giving them their first opportunity to enter the property. Firefighter John Campbell then instructed his team to don breathing apparatus and explore the smouldering house.

After finding the children first, they carried them outside and, believing they were suffering from smoke inhalation, they commenced the process of mouth-to-mouth resuscitation. It was during their attempts to revive the children that the firemen quickly realised that the children had suffered some appalling injuries, and that what at first had appeared to be a tragic accident was rapidly turning into a multiple murder.

The police were called to attend the scene, and so began a massive police inquiry that would cost millions and, in so doing, would uncover a story of lust, lesbian love, hate and murder. A complex web of relationships would have to be untangled before the true killer could be brought to justice. A web that would initially lead police to suspect members of their own force.

When the police had arrived at the house, they secured the area until Forensic Science Service (FSS) scientists were able to commence a full forensic examination. An FSS spokesman at the time said, 'One of the first priorities was to interpret the scene and try to work out what had happened and in what order. This was no mean feat. There were four sets of fires and extensive bloodstaining upstairs. Downstairs, there was bloodstaining recovered from videos in the front room, and what appeared to be a bloodstained handprint on the carpet. In the bathroom, there was blood on the shower, as though someone had made an attempt to clean themselves.'

Scientists also found hand marks in blood on other parts of the carpets and other items found in the home. In total, they were able to isolate 150 finger, palm and shoe marks.

A bloodstained sock was also found at the scene and it was thought the killer had worn the socks on his hands when committing the crimes. Scientists spent some considerable time looking at that exhibit and carried out some experimental work that showed some of the marks could have been made if the sock was worn as a glove.

Among the burned-out debris, the FSS scientists also recovered a gold jewellery chain, an item that would, in due course, play a major role in identifying the murderer.

After further examination of the scene and the bodies, more revelations emerged regarding the fires. Mrs Dawson had been set alight in bed, where she had been attacked. Mandy Power, following her murder and subsequent sexual interference, was wrapped in paper and set alight. The killer was making every effort to destroy any evidence at its source and, in this case, that meant the two adult bodies.

Once again, the investigation saw the introduction of DNA LCN analysis and SGM*plus*™, all of which would have a significant impact on the investigation. SGM*plus*™ was first introduced in September 1999 and increased the reliability of DNA anlyisis to an accuracy of one in a billion, and it was a significant improvement on the original format of SGM, which had a reliability of one in 50 million.

Mandy Power's body was found half-naked and a pathology report concluded that she had been assaulted, after death, with a sex aid. Further examination also revealed that Mandy had suffered a terrible onslaught, during which a total of 38 injuries had been inflicted. Each victim had met a gruesome end and they had all suffered crushed skulls, testament to the power behind the wielding of a long heavy pole. The police had now identified all of the victims who had lost their lives that night, and now they started to piece together the jigsaw that made up their lives, for somewhere in there they were likely to find the culprit. In the days that followed, it was Mrs Power's love life that would become the focus of the investigation.

Described by everyone as a loving and caring mother, Mrs Power had a complex and convoluted personal life, which the police increasingly saw as the key to finding the killer. She was known to have had several relationships – with both men and women – since the break-up of her marriage, but was thought to have been in a stable lesbian relationship with a former police officer called Alison Lewis at the time of her death.

To complicate matters further, Mrs Lewis was, at the time, married to a serving police officer, Sergeant Steve Lewis. His twin brother, Stuart Lewis, was also a serving police officer, and was the first person on the scene after the arrival of the fire service.

Mrs Power, who had what was best described as a varied taste in sex, and who by others was thought to be a sexual adventurer, had confided in her sister, Julie Evans, that she was enjoying a lesbian relationship with Mrs Lewis.

Previously, she had apparently enjoyed the company of

a number of men and women and was known to have kept an 'open house'. After she met Lewis, she told friends she was no longer interested in men.

After marrying Michael Power in the mid-1980s, they set up home in the close-knit Swansea Valley village of Clydach. The couple had two children but, by 1996, the marriage was effectively over and she moved into rented accomodation at Kelvin Close with the children.

A friend commented, 'She seemed to go wild after the break-up of her marriage to Michael. It was as if she was trying to make up for lost ground, cramming as much excitement into her life as she possibly could.'

After the split, Michael returned home to live with his mother, while Mandy struck up a relationship with taxi driver Richard Franks. This didn't last and, for a brief period, she was reconciled with her husband, before the marriage finally broke down completely. At the time, she blamed the breakdown of the marriage on money problems and Michael's love of golf.

Almost immediately after the final split, she took up with Michael's golfing partner, Howard Florence, himself a married man, before having another fling with neighbour Robert Wachowski. This was then followed by a short romance with a younger man, Martin Monkford, before eventually entering into an intense lesbian liaison with Alison Lewis.

A former member of the South Wales Police Constabulary, Alison had forged for herself an impressive career in sport. A karate champion, she had represented Great Britain and Wales, before turning her attention to rugby, where she also excelled, winning seven caps for the Welsh women's international rugby team. A mother of three-year-old twins, it was during her rugby-playing period that Alison fully acknowledged her own sexual orientation.

The two women met after Mandy took an interest in women's rugby and became a keen spectator at the matches. She met Alison after they were introduced through a member of the Ystradgynlais team in the Swansea Valley. Less than a week later, the pair began a lesbian relationship. Friends have reported that they could not keep their hands off each other, and that every time they met they ended up in bed. Mandy, who had been uncertain about her feelings towards women, threw herself into the relationship. Over the weeks that followed, they exchanged love tokens and chose a 'special' song together, their favourite Aerosmith track called 'Don't Want to Miss a Thing', the theme tune from the film *Armageddon*. Mandy told a friend she was like 'a silly litle girl in love'. More often than not, their liaisons were carried out under Mandy's roof, with her invalid mother in the room next door.

She also enjoyed a part-time job at a local care home, and divided her time between her busy social life, looking after her two children and caring for her mother Doris. Mandy's three older sisters – Margaret Jewell, Julie Evans and Sandra Jones – had all reported how happy and contented Mandy had been in the days before her death, although Sandra, Mandy's eldest sister, had always believed that her switch to lesbianism was 'a cry for help'.

However, the relationship was far from smooth and Alison reportedly broke it off in the early stages, alarmed at the sudden intensity, but they resumed their passion again soon afterwards. The women split again just two months before the murders, following Alison's discovery that a bizzare claim Mandy had made was false. For some reason, Mandy had told Alison that she had been diagnosed with cervical cancer, a situation which was later proven not to be true. Why she ever made this claim is not known, but family members afterwards have intimated that Mandy was confused and seeking more attention, and maybe she believed the threat imposed by such a condition would intensify the relationship further. Whatever the reason, within a week, the women were back together again and appeared to be happier than ever.

Beyond the normal trials of any relationship, and even including the hoax cancer claims, those who knew the pair have said there is no denying their need for each other. And the relationship was not one-sided, despite all of Mandy's intensity. Alison Lewis could be jealous and possessive, and was known to suffer extreme mood swings.

All in all, the two women enjoyed an exciting love life, making love whenever possible, and even making love at Mrs Lewis's house while her husband, Stephen, was asleep upstairs. It was the intricacy of the two women's relationship that was initially to form the focal point of the police investigation. When the police found out that Mandy was having an illicit love affair with an ex-colleague of theirs, in line with standard procedure they needed to rule her in or out of the inquiry. A love tryst can, and is often found to be, the melting pot from which a strong motive can be found for the committing of an offence. Therefore, Alison Lewis was a person whom the police were keen to meet.

Another person whom the police interviewed was David George Morris. He was interviewed within ten days of the offence. A known local hard man, he was also known to have had a brief liaison with Mandy and was also identified as having been in a pub in the village on the day of the murders. Witnesses said that Morris had drunk around eight pints of strong lager during the evening, and had also injected himself with a quantity of amphetamine sulphate.

In response to questions from the police, Morris said he had left the pub in Clydach at around 11.30pm, a fact supported by the landlord, and had returned home before midnight to his girlfriend, Mandy Jewell, who also confirmed this to have been the case. Mandy Jewell and Mandy Power had been quite close, but had fallen out after she, too, found out that the cervical cancer claims were false. The condition proved a little closer to home for Miss Jewell – her mother had died of the disease. Morris had also resented the closeness of their relationship, and had been pleased when it had come to an end. It was said that he disliked Mrs Power intensely, yet found her extremely attractive and had sought a sexual relationship with her.

So with Morris's alibi apparently firm, the police returned to their main suspects, Stephen and Alison Lewis. Alison was now forced to admit to Stephen that she had been involved in a serious lesbian relationship with Mandy Power. He had stated that he knew nothing of the affair, such knowledge potentially giving him a motive for the attack. Although shocked at his wife's revelation, and now fully aware of the lies she had told in order to spend nights away with Mandy, Mr Lewis stated that, on the night of the murders, Mrs Lewis had been asleep upstairs in the family home.

The police, however, were still convinced that one of them was the likely murderer, with the emphasis being on Alison Lewis. Alison had been a former British karate champion, was strong, determined and had a particular skill in the use of a long wooden pole known as a '*bo*', a weapon that had some similarity to the iron bar used in the killings.

The police sought to discover more about the two women, and of their movements and interactions in the days leading up to the massacre. Alison described the relationship as very close, loving and, above all, stable. They were very physical, and if they met ten times they would make love nine times. Whenever it was possible they would make love, usually at Mandy's house and, occasionally, at her own home. The day before the murders, she said they had had sex at her own home, while her husband was asleep upstairs. They had last had sex on the day of the murder at Lewis's home in Pontardawe, while her husband was at work.

Mrs Lewis said, 'I went into Mandy's room and she was awake. I think we fell asleep in her room. We slept for about an hour and then we went into my bedroom and made love again.'

Later that day, Mrs Lewis visited a gym before going to Mandy's house where she was washed by her lover. 'It wasn't a sexual thing, it was a caring thing,' she said, before relaying the moment she found out about the tragedy. She received a phone call early the following morning from a neighbour of Mrs Power's.

'To begin with, I thought she was drunk, she was so distressed. She kept saying, "I'm so sorry, I am so sorry." I asked her what was wrong and she said, "There's been a fire." I asked her where Mandy was, and she said, "I am so sorry."'

Mrs Lewis said she then drove down to Clydach, where she could see that the Power family home was ablaze. Getting out of the car, she asked the onlookers if they knew where Mandy was. She could not take in the enormity of the situation, or the terrible news that Mandy was dead.

Following the murders, Mrs Lewis had suffered a severe bout of depression and, at one point, had tried to commit suicide by jumping from her bedroom window. Her husband, Stephen, arrived in time to pull her back, and a day later she was admitted to a psychiatric unit in Swansea.

The police continued extensive investigations, pulling in some 60 detectives to work on the case. Anyone who knew, or had any involvement with any of the people involved in the case were interviewed but, apart from a complex series of relationships, nothing new emerged. The police had sought the owner of the gold chain, accusing David Morris of having dropped it there, but he had repeatedly denied ever having owned the chain, a fact that was again confirmed by his girlfriend Mandy Jewell.

A year passed and the inquiry seemed to be heading down a cul de sac. The police still had their doubts and suspicions regarding Alison Lewis. She and Mandy had had a passionate relationship and Alison was known to be possessive, but there was no known motive. Perhaps, they surmised, Mandy had tried to break off the relationship or had been in the company of some other partner. Mr Lewis, who had been suspended from duty during the period of the investigation, had the most likely motive.

He was, after all, the spurned husband, but he had always denied knowledge of the affair.

In an interview with the *South Wales Evening Post*, the detective leading the hunt for the killer spoke of his personal sorrow that the murderer had not been found and brought to justice. DS Martyn Lloyd Evans said he was most upset by recent criticism of the murder inquiry and urged people to pull together and support the investigation. The newspaper also reported that local councillors had called for changes in the investigation team, but Mr Evans told them that 58 officers were now working on the case, around the clock. Speaking at the time, he said, 'My officers have given a year of their lives to this investigation. Yes, they read the newspaper reports and are saddened, but we are all determined to continue. We should all be working together to solve this case.'

In its editorial section, the paper backed Mr Evans, saluting the determination his team were showing under growing public impatience.

In a bid to try and crack the case, the police arrested Mr and Mrs Lewis, on suspicion of the killing of Mandy Power, some 12 months after the murders. Mrs Lewis described the arrest, saying, 'I heard running up the stairs, my bedroom door flew open, and there were police everywhere. They came into my bedroom and told me I was under arrest for murder.' She was handcuffed and taken out on to the landing and there, in front of her daughter, the officers put plastic bags over her hands. She was then taken to the police station. But after being questioned for four days, the two were released without charge.

At the same time, Mr Lewis's twin brother, Inspector

Stewart Lewis, was arrested on suspicion of perverting the course of justice. Lewis was the first police officer on the scene of the crime and his handling of the situation was, at best, dubious. Stewart was on duty at the time of the murders, yet he could not account for his movements at the time they were committed. He did not write about this in his notebook until two days later, and then his entries appear to have been altered. When Stewart got to the scene, firemen and paramedics told him the victims had not died as a result of the fire, but had been attacked. The bodies, which had been recovered from the house, were covered in blood. Yet, instead of contacting the control room and his senior colleagues to set a murder inquiry in motion, for what appeared to be a mass murder, he disappeared for an hour instead. As a result, the house was not secured, and valuable time for the start of the forensic enquiries was lost. The force realised the seriousness of the issue only when other night-duty officers who had been at the scene returned to their base at the end of the shift. His temporary absence at the scene of a crime of such magnitude was inexplicable, and could only add to the suspicion surrounding the involvement of the Lewis family.

Throughout all of the enquiries relating to the murders, nothing concrete was found in respect of any of the suspects. The FSS had not collected any DNA material from the scene. If there had been any there, it would have been destroyed in the fire and then washed away in the firemen's attempts to bring the flames under control.

The case was yielding little in the way of positive breaks. And then some news arrived that would give the case fresh impetus and a new direction. The gold chain was the only item that had been found at the scene that did not belong there; it was therefore generally accepted to have been left by the murderer. In a slip-up, David Morris admitted to his cousin, Eric Williams, that the gold chain found at the scene was, in fact, his. Unfortunately, Mr Williams then mentioned this to a friend, who, in turn, told an off-duty police officer. Morris was immediately elevated from being a 'person of interest' to a strong suspect. He was arrested in March 2001, and charged with four counts of murder.

Morris's background was now scrutinised as the police sought to examine the details of their new key suspect. Morris had, in fact, been convicted of a string of offences, which included violent robbery of a woman and hitting a man over the head with a piece of wood during a brawl. He also had convictions for car theft, benefit fraud and fighting in a pub and had been in jail for four years.

He had also got away with another violent incident, during which one of his neighbours, Mr Carl Wessel, was beaten about the head with a solid implement, causing him skull damage. Someone had described Morris as beating Mr Wassel 'within an inch of his life'. Fortunately for Morris, the case was dropped when none of the witnesses turned up at court, perhaps another insight into the influence Morris was able to wield in his own district. Morris had also claimed a previous sexual relationship with Mandy Power, who was said to have been afraid of Morris because of his violent past. It was while he was in jail that Morris obtained the gold chain in a 'swap' deal with another prisoner. However, during the course of these interviews, Morris continued to deny that the chain was his.

FSS scientists then analysed the chain more thoroughly. It had, of course, been through a fire and what subsequently amounted to a flood, yet there, embedded within the links, the FSS scientists found a tiny amount of green paint. Officers were despatched to Morris's address, where a full search was undertaken. It was here that the officers noted that Morris's kitchen had green kitchen units. It was a long shot, but a small amount of the paint was taken for analysis. Sure enough, the results were positive, and the chain was proven to be definintely linked to or probably belonged to Mr Morris.

Faced with what appeared to be irrefutable evidence, Morris was forced to rethink his story. He finally admitted that the chain belonged to him, but claimed that he had left it there a few days before the murder. He said he had put it down on a kitchen work surface while he and Mandy had sex, a story that the police did not entirely believe.

Morris's defence deteriorated further when his girlfriend, Mandy Jewell, changed her statement in respect of Morris's movements on the night of the murder. Whether this was in response to his new claims of having had sex with Mrs Power is not known, although she now stated that Morris was not in the house by midnight, but had, in fact, returned some time between 3.00am and 4.00am. On that evening, they had gone out together for a drink but, as Morris became more drunk, an argument broke out and Miss Jewell returned to the house by herself.

The case against Morris was strengthening by the day and the CPS were now ready to test the evidence in court. The time of reckoning was fast approaching for David

'Dai' Morris, although the courtroom itself would be the scene of more conflicting stories, and the emergence of new facts, which would show that maybe all those involved had not been entirely honest. Yet it was the freedom of David Morris that was at stake. It was he who was in the dock.

When the case finally came to court, the jurors were sworn in and the trial judge, Mr Justice Butterfield, outlined the charges against Morris, to which he pleaded not guilty. The prosecuting counsel, Patrick Harrington QC, then made his opening statements, which effectively described the case against Mr Morris. It was stated that, on the night of the murders, Mr Morris had been at a pub not far from where the murders occurred. There he had consumed a large amount of strong lager and had also injected himself with an amphetamine drug. He was heard by others in the bar to have spoken loudly and in an aggresive way about Mrs Power. He had then argued with his girlfriend who had left.

Later on, Morris had gone to Mrs Power's house hoping to have sex, but was turned down. In a drunken, drug-fuelled rage, he had battered the occupants of the house to death, and then attempted to destroy the evidence by setting the house on fire. To add weight to the prosecution's claims, a gold chain belonging to Morris was found at the scene of the crime, a chain he denied owning until forensic evidence proved otherwise, and there had been a catalogue of lies and denials made by Morris during the investigation. And in further support of the prosecution's case, Morris had no firm alibi, his original one now having been withdrawn by his girlfriend who was, however, still supporting him.

After all the elapsed time, it now looked like the case was pretty much cut and dried, yet there was other evidence to be heard that would not make the decision to convict David Morris an easy one. The general case for the defence was summarised in the following way. Following such a horrific attack, the FSS team had been unable to locate any forensic material belonging to Morris at the scene of the crime. The prosecution were also unable to disprove that the chain, belonging to Morris, had been left there on a previous visit; this was significant, as the chain was one of the key links in the case for the prosecution. And there was no known motive that anyone could identify that would result in such an outpouring of bloody destruction.

But the defence also had a number of other observations to make that might get the jurors thinking twice before convicting Morris. A Miss Williams was produced, who claimed to have seen a man walking quickly away from the scene at the time of the attack. She said she was returning from Cardiff after a night out when she saw the man, described as about 6ft tall. She slowed to take a closer look at the man to see if it was someone she knew. She did not know him, but described him as wearing a police-style bomber jacket. The police asked her to complete an E-fit photograph, which eventually bore a remarkable resemblance to Stephen Lewis, a man who could be said to have had a motive, as it was his wife who was having an affair with Mandy Power. Miss Williams was later able to pick Lewis out at an identity parade.

Lewis was also having problems explaining his movements on the night of the murder, although he was not the one in the dock. However, the defence wanted to demonstrate sufficient doubt, so as to make a conviction unsafe.

Mr Harrington, responding for the prosecution, vigorously pursued Miss Williams. She regularly took an aerobics class at a local leisure centre that was also regularly attended by Lewis. Surely she would have recognised him if she had seen him clearly, as she had suggested?

During forensic analysis of the murder scene, the FSS had identified and isolated a number of bloody handprints. Although these do not share the same unique identifying characteristics as a fingerprint, they can add weight to a case providing they can be shown to be more or less likely to belong to a suspect. The defence called on the expertise of ex-Detective Inspector Swann, an authority on fingerprinting, who claimed that the handprint did not belong to David Morris, but that it was a better fit to the hand shape of Alison Lewis.

The defence also concentrated on the way in which the victims had been attacked, with a long pole. The defence now called in another ex-police officer and martial arts expert, Mick Finn, who explained how the injuries could have been inflicted by someone who was trained in martial arts. Mr Finn then demonstrated in court, with the use of a broom handle, how the weapon may have been wielded. Once again, Alison Lewis was back in the firing line because of her known skill with the '*bo*'.

Many photographs and much video footage was taken of the crime scene as the police sought to capture as much visual evidence as they could. The court now decided that the jurors should see for themselves the carnage that had occurred on that evening. It would not make pleasant viewing, as the images showed in graphic detail the terror of what had really gone on. During the course of the viewing, two jurors felt ill, one fainting and requiring hospital treatment. The case had to be temporarily halted while two new jurors were sworn in and, at end of the trial, the judge discharged the men and women from any further jury duty, ruling that they had seen more than anyone should have to do in one lifetime.

As the trial progressed, the prosecution continued to press home the significance of the gold chain. Assuming that Morris had left it there on a previous visit, why had it been found just inches away from the body of Mandy Power, who was killed in one of the bedrooms? This fact was certainly significant and the defence could only suggest it was mere coincidence and that it did not prove anything.

In due course, the defence were able to find a witness who was able to throw significant doubt on Morris's guilt. The trouble was, the witness had come to light during the course of the trial, and had produced information that she had somehow forgotten 12 months earlier when she had first been interviewed. Louise Pugh, aged 19, was the neighbour of Mandy Power in Kelvin Road. She claimed that, on the night of the murders, she had posted back through Mandy Power's letterbox a film that she had previously borrowed. She said she had done this just hours before the massacre took place. That same video had subsequently turned up at the home of Alison Lewis. Again, the defence were hoping to demonstrate that others in the courtroom, although not in the dock, may have been more likely than Morris to have committed the murders.

Alison Lewis also took the stand and sobbed when

asked whether she had murdered Mandy Power, her daughters and her 80-year-old mother – she denied it. She explained to the jury that she had been through four days of hell as the police questioned her about the killings. Morris's defence team would continue throughout the trial to insist that it was more likely that Lewis was, in fact, the guilty party. Peter Rouch QC for the defence suggested that, as a previous karate champion and an expert *'bo'* user, it was Mrs Lewis who fitted the bill better than any of the other suspects.

The village was split – half the population believed in Morris's innocence and the others believed he was a man capable of murder. Campaigners on behalf of Morris visited pubs in the South Wales village in an attempt to get a petition signed to support his claim of innocence. However, the guilt or otherwise of David Morris rested entirely on a simple proposition – that he had left his chain at the scene of the murder, that he had no alibi for his movements at the time of the murder, that he had been drunk and high on drugs at the time of the murder, that he was known to have harboured a severe dislike for Mandy Power while maintaining a sexual lust for her and, finally, that he had a string of convictions and complaints against him, many of which demonstrated his penchant and capacity for violence. And as an ex-con, he would have been forensically aware, hence the attempt to destroy the available evidence by starting the fire.

Finally, the jury were given the benefit of the judge's summary and were asked to retire to consider their verdict. After an 11-week trial, the jury took just 12 hours to come back with a decision. In a 10–2 majority, the jury voted in favour of a guilty verdict, and the longest investigation ever in South Wales was brought to a close.

The defendant stood stony-faced as the verdict was delivered, but cries of jubilation from the Dawson family were matched by shouts of anger from Morris's family in the public gallery. Several members of whom, including his mother Shirley and father Brian, held their faces in their hands as shouts of 'bastard' were heard around the court.

Butterfield looked directly at Morris and sentenced him to four life sentences, one for each charge. He told him, 'These were horrific murders committed with great savagery on four defenceless victims. You have shown not a trace of compassion or sympathy for the terrible injuries you have inflicted.'

Mr Justice Butterfield then looked directly at Morris and said, 'I am sentencing you to four counts of life, one for each charge. Now take him down.'

6

WILL THE REAL MR PLATT...?

In July 1996, the trawler Malkerry was bobbing about in the gentle swell of the English Channel, some six miles off the coast of Brixham. The crew and owners of the fishing vessel were a father-and-son team, John and Craig Topik.**

It had been a generally uneventful day, having managed to yield little in the way of a worthwhile catch and they had been out at sea for ten hours already. The fishing net trailed along behind the boat, somewhere near to the seabed, as they pulled it along hoping to entrap a shoal of fish.

Suddenly, something heavy pulled at the net. The two men thought they had snagged an underwater object, or more probably a porpoise had swum into it and was now struggling to find a way out. Experienced as they were, they could tell by the behaviour of the net, and the boat, that the catch was not a shoal of fish, but a single, heavy item, and both considered a porpoise the most likely candidate. A shoal of fish would gently take up the slack in the net guide ropes as one, then tens, then hundreds of fish would be dragged along. They would have to pull the net in and release the sea creature, if that is what it was.

Wearily, they started to wind the net back aboard, aware that more valuable fishing time was being lost. The day would turn out to be a complete disaster if they didn't find a suitable catch soon. The net was finally hoisted over the side of the boat and, as the water ran away, the two fishermen were stunned, gaping at the contents of their net. Within the criss-cross of the netting, the body of a man lay tangled, fully clothed, with a bloated, pale face. The surprised fishermen quickly made a ship-to-shore call to the police and reported their find.

On closer inspection, Mr Topik Sr could see that a sizeable boat anchor had been secured through the belt of the dead man's trousers. This was no accident; indeed, it was the start of an investigation that would eventually reveal a grisly tale of murder, fraud and the stealing of another man's identity.

The police stood on the dock and waited for the *Malkerry* to berth. The fishermen had been told not to interfere with the body, but to head immediately for home, where officers would meet them. At the same time, enquiries made at the local lifeboat stations failed to turned up a record of any missing persons. At that time, the police were unaware of the anchor attached to the unidentified man.

Once the trawler arrived at the dockside, the corpse was removed to the security of the police mortuary and efforts were made to determine the dead man's identity, which proved to be a most difficult task. The man's pockets had all been turned out, he had no wallet on him and no identifying tags were attached to any of his clothing. Confused, the police turned to the only other two unique distinguishing features that might shed some light on the situation. The dead man did have a tattoo on the back of his right hand; and just above it, on his wrist, was a heavy, Oyster Perpetual gold Rolex watch.

For the moment, the tattoo was of no use in making a positive identification, but could prove to be useful in due course as a source of final confirmation by someone who could identify it.

However, the police had a rather inspired thought. Rolex watches, like the one worn by the dead man, cost thousands of pounds and would be identified individually by serial number. When enquiring with Rolex, they were told that each watch is separately identifiable and that the provision of the number would locate the jeweller who had sold it. His receipts might then identify the man – that is, assuming he was the legitimate owner.

The subsequent investigations proved most rewarding as the watch was tracked to a jeweller in Harrogate, North Yorkshire, and from there a name emerged. It would appear that the man dredged up from the Channel was one Ronald Platt, a 51-year-old television repair man. Notably, the watch had stopped at 11.35 on 22 July 1996. Given that it was known the watch had a 40-hour run capacity from the point of the last full wind, this then indicated a potential date of death of around 20 July. Gradually, small facts were emerging that would now, through a series of chance encounters, lead to a fascinating and extraordinary story.

It took some time after the discovery of the body before forensic and circumstantial evidence pointed irrevocably towards foul play. In addition to the obviously attached anchor, Mr Platt had a rather deep and nasty gash on the back of his head. The gash, although sufficient to render the man unconscious, was not the cause of death. The coroner's verdict was that death had been caused by drowning. Through the Rolex connection, police were confident they had identified the dead man as Ronald Platt, though more details about the victim and his life – and death – were slow to emerge.

Almost a month after the discovery of the body, the police traced the address of a flat that Platt had been renting in Chelmsford. The flat at this stage was the only link the police had, but fortunately the landlord and owner of the premises was able to provide another, seemingly tenuous link. The landlord stated that the flat had been rented to Mr Platt, who had provided a Mr David Davis as a reference and, in a further stroke of luck, Mr Davis had kindly written his mobile telephone number on the rental agreement.

The police called the number and broke the bad news to Mr Davis that his associate was dead. Davis confirmed that Mr Platt had been his best friend and that he had last seen him alive in June – he was, by all accounts, shocked and upset by the news.

This may have been the end of the enquiry as far as Davis's involvement went, but for another fortunate turn of events. The police had some final ends to tie up with Davis and thought a personal visit, rather than another telephone call, might be preferable. To this end, the Devon and Cornwall Constabulary asked their colleagues from Chelmsford to call on Davis to conclude the questioning.

DS Frank Redman of Essex CID was despatched to the farmhouse address to handle the matter. He had been fully briefed on the Ronald Platt case and was of the mind that Mr Davis was a friend of the victim and not a suspect in what was obviously a gruesome murder. On arrival in the area, Redman found that there were four farmhouses, all scattered down an unsurfaced, typical farmer's lane. He drove slowly down the bumpy road but could not identify the house, known as 'Little London Farmhouse'. In fact, none of the houses were identifiable by either name or number. Parking his car, Redman decided to proceed on foot and visit the middle house of the four. Knocking on the door of the farmhouse, he was greeted by the elderly owner, Mr Frank Johnson.

'Could you tell me if this is Little London Farmhouse?' asked Redman.

'No, it's not,' replied Mr Johnson. 'Little London Farmhouse is over there.' He pointed across the lane to another house, partly obscured by trees.

'And is that where a Mr Davis lives?' asked Redman.

'Wrong again,' smiled Mr Johnson. 'That is where Mr Platt lives, with his lovely young wife Noelle.'

Unknowingly, Mr Davis had risen from the rank of Friend of Victim to that of Chief Suspect. DS Redman needed to revise his plan of attack.

On 31 October, shortly after breakfast, Davis jumped into a taxi in which he intended to travel to Chelmsford. At the end of the lane, however, the taxi was brought to a standstill by a range of police vehicles, backed up by an armed response unit. Davis was ordered out of the taxi, as

DS Redman stepped forward. 'Mr Davis, I am arresting you on suspicion of the murder of Ronald Platt, in Devon on or around 21 July 1996.

Mr Davis was whisked away to the police station, while officers holding a search warrant for the address entered the farmhouse and were astounded by what they uncovered. Hidden in various places were bags filled with money. One group of bags contained some £30,000 in sterling and Swiss Francs. In another part of the house, they found a stack of gold bars, again worth many thousands. In one room, the police found a young lady, calling herself Noelle Davis, who had been in the process of putting yet more cash into a bag.

The police did not know what to make of the situation. After all, it is not a crime to store money or valuables at your address, providing, of course, you are the legal owner. However strange the scene looked, the police were not aware of any robbery; they were there to find evidence connecting Davis to the murder of Ronald Platt.

Back at the station, the police had identified Davis as a Canadian citizen and, as a standard procedure and courtesy, they contacted the Canadian High Commission in London to inform them that they had arrested one of their countrymen on suspicion of murder. Once again, the police were provided with a chance piece of information that would shed more light on the case. The police had supplied the Canadian authorities with Davis's fingerprints and the resulting match told a completely different story. The prints were those of another Canadian called Albert Walker, who was also on Interpol's list of most wanted criminals for serious fraud offences. David Wallis Davis was an alias used by Walker to avoid detection by the authorities.

And so the police were now holding a man whose neighbours knew him as Ronald Platt, who more usually operated under the alias David W Davis, but who, in reality, was the very much wanted Mr Albert Walker – a big-time swindler from Canada.

The story of Albert Walker begins with his birth in August 1945 in the predominantly steel-producing town of Hamilton, Ontario. His parents were small-time farmers, yet Walker always harboured ideas of escaping to a more prosperous life. In his later years, he would often pour scorn over his parents' lowly social status, claiming that he had risen above them.

As a young man, he spent a large part of his time hanging around the social scene at Ontario's University of Waterloo. It was there, at a dance, that he met Barbara McDonald. He proposed within a few days and they eventually married in 1968, starting a family almost straight away. They had three daughters and a son and settled down to their lives.

On the face of it, Walker seemed a pillar of the community. A church elder and Sunday school teacher, he had the complete trust of his local community, a trust that could be exploited when he finally started an investment business with his wife. Using those who regarded him as a friend, he quickly managed to invest nearly $3m Canadian dollars (£1.27 million) into savings bonds. With the help of pensioners' savings and other investments, this amount later swelled to nearly $12m Canadian dollars (£5 million).

This provided Walker with an executive lifestyle; he wore designer clothes, dined in the top restaurants and even bought a new Jaguar motor car. At the same time, he also started to create a new past for himself. By his own account, he had been educated at Oxford University and held a professorship at a leading Canadian institution. The truth is that Walker had not even completed a secondary school education, failing to graduate from the rural school he attended in Ontario.

His lifestyle blossomed and he began travelling first-class throughout Canada, Britain and Switzerland, while at the same time presenting the image of a loving family man. But his marriage, too, had become a sham and Walker had commenced a series of extra-marital affairs, which eventually cost him his marriage when Barbara found out. As his marriage collapsed, he took the decision to move out of the family home, taking his four children with him, but a subsequent custody battle saw the two youngest children, Duncan and Heather, being returned to their mother.

As relations between the two deteriorated, Barbara was incensed to discover that Walker had paid for their eldest daughter to have breast enlargements, and at the same time had helped Sheena, his 15-year-old daughter, to obtain a birth-control prescription.

Their relationship deteriorated further when Barbara decided to stop Walker having access to his two youngest children at all. Things seemed to be getting more and more difficult for Walker and, on top of his domestic troubles, his colleagues in his investment firm were increasingly alarmed at the continual extravagance of Walker's lifestyle. He was now constantly being asked to provide answers as to where all the funds were invested. The answers he provided never seemed satisfactory and so pressure was being exerted to uncover the truth.

The date 4 November 1990 marked a turning point in Walker's life, and one that would eventually lead to murder. In a desperate bid to see his children, Walker attempted to kick in the front door of the family home, while the terrified Barbara contacted the police. Walker was arrested and charged with forcible entry, a minor offence but one which required him to provide his fingerprints, prints which would later help to nail him as a killer.

Walker's life was falling apart around him and the brush with the law acted as a catalyst for his next move. It was now that he decided to flee Canada, before the truth could be found out about his investment company.

In December 1990, Walker made his move. He flew from Toronto to Switzerland and then on to London, with his daughter Sheena at his side. In keeping with the lavish lifestyle he had become accustomed to, Walker and Sheena took up a suite at the posh Ritz Hotel in London. They spent the next six days living in splendid comfort, leaving behind them a trail of broken promises, false claims and worse. He had defrauded friends and colleagues out of millions, leaving some destitute, their entire futures depending on the prudent investment performance that Walker had promised.

The Ritz would be the last time Walker and Sheena would represent themselves under their real identities. Leaving the Ritz, they effectively vanished off the face of the earth.

In reality, Walker was now calling himself David Wallis Davis – in real life, one of Walker's Canadian colleagues, who had once remarked that they looked so similar they could pass for brothers. And he took it a stage further; he had stolen the real Davis's birth certificate and national insurance number and had now taken his identity as well. The information for the real Mr Davis had been easily obtained through an investment he had handled on his behalf before he had fled.

In England, the debonair, smooth-talking Davis impressed those who would listen with his tales of international travel, flying on Concorde, meeting Rod Stewart and even having a meal with the ex-President of the United States, Ronald Reagan.

A chance encounter with Elaine Boyes, a receptionist from Harrogate, would bring the dashing Mr Davis into contact with the unfortunate Ronald Platt. After their short stay at the Ritz, Walker and his daughter had travelled north to Harrogate where he had spotted a painting hanging in the window of a fine art dealership. On entering, he continued to browse. When Miss Boyes heard his distinct Canadian accent, she struck up a conversation with Walker, telling him that her boyfriend, Ronald Platt, had lived in Canada as a youngster and that he would love to move back there some day.

The scene was now set and Walker developed his plan for another new identity. A better opportunity could not have presented itself for Walker, and he grabbed it with both hands.

Walker gave Miss Boyes a brief resumé of his past. He was an international banker, who had been educated at Edinburgh University and had now decided to set up his own company. He said he had visited the art showroom because he thought he might like to sell art and possibly antiques.

By her own admission, Miss Boyes was quite taken in by the 'hypnotic' charm of David Davis, and was even more taken aback when he rapidly offered her a job with his new company at a starting salary of £15,000 per year, as a receptionist. Although reluctant at first, she accepted the job and the two began to see more of each other as they started the business.

Walker introduced Miss Boyes to his young daughter Sheena, who was now calling herself Noelle and parading herself as Walker's wife. Social evenings were arranged and Walker was always particularly careful to include Ronald Platt in the proceedings. One weekend, he took them all to London and spent £400 on a lavish meal.

Miss Boyes recalls that her new boss was a man of many ideas, wanting to sell antiques and art one minute, but then suggesting they open a tea room or contemplating buying a corner shop. There was a lot of talk, but, other than buying and selling a few antiques, not a lot else happened. More and more, Walker indulged Boyes and Platt in discussions on a move to Canada, something which Platt seemed very taken with.

At Christmas 1992, Walker's plan to assume another identity moved a step closer and, with it, Walker's disappearance for ever. Walker invited Boyes and Platt to a social gathering at the house he shared in Harrogate with Noelle. There he unveiled his present to them; he promised to buy plane tickets to Canada for them both, so that they could set up a new life. They could still maintain their interest in the antiques business, of which both Miss Boyes and Platt were now directors.

Platt, who had lived in Canada for eight years from the age of ten, was astounded at Walker's generosity and looked upon the gift as a wonderful opportunity to get his life back on track in a country that he had loved as a child.

Whether he had any idea at this stage that his identity was being stripped away is not known.

Before leaving for Canada, both Boyes and Platt opened accounts in the UK to allow Walker to use them for the purposes of carrying out company business. He also, somehow, managed to persuade Platt to allow him to use his birth certificate and driving licence while he was away, a move that, in due course, would cost him his life.

As the time approached for them to fly to Canada, Boyes was overtaken by a sudden feeling of doubt and demanded the tickets be return flights, just in case. And with that, the couple set off to start a new life together, leaving their friend behind, with everything he needed to assume his new identity.

Once in Canada, the couple experienced a number of challenges. Neither had particularly planned on the blizzard conditions of the Canadian winter, which at times saw temperatures dropping to as low as -35°C. Platt, who had previously trained as a TV repairman and had been a soldier in the Signals Corp, was now finding it difficult to get a job.

The strain, eventually, became too much and, when Boyes paid a flying visit to the UK in July 1993, she decided she could not return to Canada. Reacquainting herself with Walker, she later recalled how he had spent time trying to persuade her to go back, saying that 'you owe it to Ron to give it another chance'.

The persuasion ploy didn't work and Boyes remained in the UK. Then, in a final twist, in the summer of 1995, Platt himself returned to the UK, disillusioned at not being able to sustain suitable employment; by doing so, he virtually signed his own death warrant.

By the time of Platt's return, Walker and Sheena were living in a rented farmhouse in Woodham Walter, Essex. Interestingly, Sheena had also given birth to her second child, although she was not known to have a boyfriend and was still masquerading as the wife of the Canadian conman.

Platt's return was a real problem for Walker, who had all but consumed the other's identity. Clearly, two Mr Platts was one too many, and the real one was the one that would have to be dealt with.

For a year following Platt's return, Walker supported him and, on many occasions, tried to persuade him that his life would be better back in Canada, where the cost of living was less and the exchange rate better. Platt, however, had been put off by his inability to land an appropriate role and had now decided that, for the time being at least, he would remain in the UK ... with his good friend.

Walker continued to support Platt, providing money to live on and also securing him rented accommodation. It is still not known if Platt was aware of the other's ongoing impersonation of him. What is believed, though, is that Walker was once again starting to feel the heat. In order to progress with his sham, only one Mr Platt could be allowed to live in the UK, and having two living so close by in Essex was likely to cause problems in due course.

During this period, Walker once again hatched another plan, this time to rid himself of the problem once and for all. Walker decided to take Platt on a holiday down in Devon, where he had a boat moored called the *Lady Jane*.

In typical Walker fashion, he now had to spin a different yarn to a number of different people and take a rearguard action to provide a cover for his increasingly criminal behaviour. Walker now told Sheena that Platt would be moving away to France in order to run a business that the two had set up. It would be a very busy time for Platt and they should not expect to see him for quite some time.

At the same time, Walker, in a brazen move, booked himself and Platt into a public house in Devon as a holiday break for the pair, during which they would be able to relax on the *Lady Jane*, moored close by.

Walker also decided to take Sheena with him, and booked a cottage close to the pub, in Dittisham. This was a risky move, as the distance between the pub and the cottage could have given rise to the individuals bumping into each other. It is therefore a testament to the extreme arrogance and confidence that Walker displayed over this period, and this same attitude would come to pervade his behaviour in the courtroom, when he would finally be brought to trial.

Walker and Sheena arrived in Devon earlier than Platt, so Walker was able to settle Sheena into the cottage before excusing himself, saying he was going out for a while and would probably have a relaxing drink before returning.

Meanwhile, he met Platt at the pub and again persuaded him to indulge in some mild cover-up. He suggested they book into the pub under the name of Platt, suggesting they represent themselves as cousins. No one will ever know why, but Platt once again consented, and the two Mr Platts were given rooms for the evening.

After an evening meal together, Walker, feigning tiredness, excused himself and said he would retire for the evening. Platt, who had had a long drive himself, agreed that an early night would be best for all, and the evening was drawn to a close.

When the coast was clear, Walker rushed back to the cottage and spent the rest of the evening with Sheena and the children, suggesting he would be off early in the morning as he intended to do a bit of sailing by himself. Sheena, of course, would not be able to go as she would have to look after the children; the *Lady Jane* would not be the sort of place for infants to be walking around.

On the morning of 20 July, Walker met Ronald Platt at the quayside, where they boarded Walker's yacht, the *Lady Jane*. The boat then headed out of the Dart Estuary and into the open waters of the English Channel. They headed directly away from the mainland and into deeper waters. The exact details of what happened next shall probably never be known, although the basic facts are clear enough. When the *Lady Jane* was about six miles out into the Channel, Walker struck Ronald Platt a severe and debilitating blow to the back of the head with an anchor he had chillingly bought for the purpose. The semi-unconscious Platt was then dragged to the edge of the boat, where Walker secured the 10lb anchor through his trouser belt. Then, in a final act of premeditated cover-up, Walker turned out Platt's pockets, looking for any item that might identify the man in the unlikely event he should be found, before pushing him overboard. Unfortunately for Walker, he had missed Platt's Rolex watch, which would be the first lucky break the police would get in identifying the dead man. Death would be caused by drowning, as the heavy anchor pulled him down to the sea bed. Platt, in his dazed state, would not even have been aware of why he was sinking and so death would have occurred within a minute or so of entering the water.

With the murder of Platt out of the way, Walker steered the *Lady Jane* back to shore and returned the craft to its mooring. No one would question Platt's disappearance as he was meant to be in France running a new business. But even at this stage there was more covering of tracks to be done. Walker now returned to the rented dwelling that Platt was using and removed all of his belongings, putting them into storage and thus adding weight to the fact that Platt had moved away.

In an amazing stroke of bad luck for Walker, Platt was eventually picked up by the Topiks' trawler and the Rolex soon identified Platt, leading, in turn, to Walker's involvement.

On trial, Walker, aged 52, was described as 'a ruthless and cunning man' by the judge at Exeter Crown Court. Mr Justice Butterfield told him, 'It was a callous, premeditated killing designed to eliminate a man you had used for your own selfish ends and found to be an inconvenience and increasingly a threat to your continued freedom. He became not only expendable but a danger to you, and he had to die. The killing was carefully planned and cunningly executed with chilling efficiency. You covered your tracks so effectively that only a merest chance led to you coming under suspicion. You are a plausible, intelligent and ruthless man, who poses a serious threat to anyone who stands in your way.'

As Walker was found guilty, police admitted that, if it had not been for the watch, they would not have been able to identify the body. However, once Walker had been cornered, the continuing police investigations led to other damning evidence being found. The *Lady Jane* was equipped with the latest in satellite navigation systems, capable of pinpointing the yacht's position on the sea to within a few metres. The system also stored historical movement data as an audit. Although Walker had been wise enough to remove the system from the boat after the murder, the equipment was eventually found on a thorough search of Walker's premises. The system data confirmed that, at 9.00pm on 20 July, the *Lady Jane* was close to where the body had been found.

Enquiries made by the police at the marina where the *Lady Jane* was moored provided more corroborating evidence. A man who had been at the harbourside that day confirmed that a man with an American-sounding accent had boarded a yacht with another man, matching the description of Ronald Platt.

Further proof was provided when the police analysed the financial records of Walker. He had foolishly bought the 10lb anchor on his own credit card a few days before the murder took place.

Forensic proof was also found after an inch-by-inch search of the *Lady Jane*, which revealed strands of Platt's hair.

On questioning Sheena Walker, she claimed to have been unaware of Platt's presence in Devon. She believed she was on holiday with her father and children. When pressed further regarding her father's sailing trip, she said, 'He said he was going out sailing alone. On his return, he said the sailing was fine and the weather was good ... that sort of thing.' Sheena said she had learned of Platt's death the following month from the police.

Following his arrest, she had spoken to her father one

last time in 1997. 'He asked me to change my statement,' she said, 'to say that I had known Ronald Platt was down in Devon. He wanted me to tell the police that I had just forgotten.' Sheena Walker was released; the court believed she had been caught up in her father's deceit, as his crime spree had started when she was just a child. Sheena and her two children have now returned to Canada and reside with her mother.

In a final, sad epitaph for Ronald Platt, the judge summed up his character: 'Mr Platt was a shy, introverted loner, who appeared to have a knack of failing at almost everything to which he turned his hand.'

Elaine Boyes provided a kinder picture of the man she had shared a part of her life with, and, unwittingly, had introduced that man to his eventual killer. 'Ron was an extremely honest, kind and gentle man. But he was conned ... we were both conned.'

In a final twist to the saga of Albert Walker, it would appear the world will continue to hear more of him. Every day during the trial, the public gallery contained an array of people from the world of television and showbusiness. Susan George and her husband Simon McCorquodale, who own a film production company in Canada, were in attendance as they were hopeful of producing a story about Walker's life of crime, and Harry Hook, the English film director, who had a front row seat in the public gallery, was also planning a movie based on the case.

7

NO PLACE TO HIDE

On the morning of Friday, 26 April 1968, the banner headline on the *Dorking Advertiser* read 'POLICE SEARCH FOR SCHOOLBOY WHO HITCHED A LIFT'.

Four days earlier, 14-year-old schoolboy Roy Tuthill had gone missing on his way home from school. Hitch-hiking, in those days, was common practice for youngsters, regardless of how risky it is considered to be today. Roy's elder brother Colin said, 'We always hitch-hiked from our home in Brockham to Kingston Grammar School, which lay 15 miles away, and then did the same on the way back. Our parents weren't comfortable with the idea, but they gradually came to accept it. There had never been any problems. I hitched to school and back every day for three years.'

His mother, Hilary Tuthill, later told a journalist, 'I had no idea that Roy was hitch-hiking. He had always been warned against it. There is no doubt that he always had sufficient fare money.'

Mrs Tuthill expected her youngest son to be home by 5.00pm. At 6.00pm, her husband Dennis arrived home and they both became anxious for his safety. They phoned friends, hospitals and police stations for news of their son without success. When two friends arrived at their house, the four retraced Roy's route between home and school, then they walked into Dorking Police Station at 9.20pm to report his disappearance.

Chief Inspector Philip Doyle, head of Dorking CID, said, 'These parents acted with commendable speed. We would always wish to receive this type of report as early as possible. We consider it far better to receive a false alarm early than a genuine report late.' Any parent reading this article should ponder those words.

Over the next three days, officers conducted house-to-house enquiries with neighbours in the village of Brockham, and pupils and teachers at Roy's school were questioned. The fact that Roy had been seen hitching a lift was established.

Most of the children who hitched did it to save their bus fares, and Roy was no different. The lad was saving up for a new train for his collection which he shared with his brother and for a new bicycle, and had been told by his parents that he could keep any money left over from his bus fares.

That morning, he had hitched a lift on his way to school. Police discovered this after two motorists came forward after the *Dorking Advertiser* ran a Missing Persons appeal in the newspaper. That Tuesday morning, one driver had given Roy a lift from Brockham, near Dorking, to Leatherhead along the A24. Another took him from Leatherhead to Kingston.

Later that day, after he left school at 3.30pm, Roy – 'Tutts' to his friends – had caught a red number 65 double-decker bus. He could have stayed on the bus all the way to Leatherhead, taken another bus or coach to Dorking, then a local bus to Brockham. Although he had just under £1 on him, he bought only a 6d fare. He left the bus at the last stop on the northern side of the Bridge Road roundabout, and walked towards the bus-stop lay-by on the opposite side, about 100 yards further along the A24. This was known by several pupils to be a good place to hitch a lift. Four roads converge at this point and anyone standing on this lay-by would have a pretty good chance of getting a lift.

The last people to see Roy – apart from his killer – had been his schoolfriend, who had stayed on the bus when he had alighted, and the bus crew. The bus conductor said the time was 3.58pm. The driver of the London Transport bus number 468 said he arrived at the Bridge Road roundabout at about 4.00pm – just two minutes after Roy had got off his own bus at that spot. The driver remembered that the traffic here was being held up by a slow-moving, immaculate-looking silver-grey Austin Westminster car.

Eventually, the car turned south on to the A24 and stopped in the bus lay-by, where the bus driver wanted to pull up. Angered by this, the bus driver deliberately blocked the driver in the lay-by. The driver of the Austin Westminster had stopped to talk to a schoolboy standing in the lay-by. As far as the driver could remember, the boy that he saw matched the description of Roy as given in the newspaper. At that point he drove on, and did not see if the boy climbed into the car, but he was able to give an accurate description of both the car and the driver.

However, a conflicting statement was provided by a woman who lived opposite the roundabout. At 4.25pm – a full 25 minutes after the bus driver said he saw Roy talking to the car driver, she claims to have spoken to Roy – she had seen him standing at that spot on previous occasions. She thought it was dangerous and told him that there were a lot of buses coming along this road, but he merely smiled at her. When she glanced out of her front window just five minutes later, the boy answering Roy's description was gone.

Shortly before 1.00pm on the same day the appeal appeared in the *Dorking Advertiser*, four forestry workers were on their way home from Lord Beaverbrook's estate – Cherkley Court Estate, at Mickleham, on the outskirts of Dorking. They had been hard at work all morning and were on their way back to their cottages for their lunch break. Passing by a cluster of beech trees, they glanced across to the copse as they often did to see if there was any wildlife present and saw the body of a young boy.

Detective Phillip Doyle of Surrey CID arrived on the scene and later described the pitiful sight. The boy lay face down on the rough earth, his bright pink-and-grey blazer slung across him which made it look 'like a beacon', as Doyle later described it. His school satchel lay beside him which contained his raincoat and school homework. He had not been robbed. An examination of his pockets revealed that he still had his change from the bus and the last bus ticket to the White Hart bus-stop was still in his wallet.

The first thing evident to DI Doyle was that the killer was a local man for two reasons. First, the appeal for the missing youngster had only just appeared that morning in the *Dorking Advertiser* and the killer must, therefore, have panicked and decided to get rid of the body immediately. Second, only a local person would have thought of dumping the schoolboy in such a secluded spot; only a local man would have known of its existence and the likelihood that no one would probably be there to witness him leaving the boy where he did.

When questioned, one of the four workers said he had peered into the copse in search of game or rabbits, and he would easily have seen the body that morning had it been there. The body lay so close to the road it was inconceivable that anyone passing the spot would have missed it. Police also noted that the grass under the body was still fresh; if the body had been there since death, then it would have been contaminated by the corpse.

Although the body had only been put there that morning, the post-mortem revealed that he had been dead for two or three days and probably died shortly after going missing on the Tuesday. The pathologist, Dr Keith Mant, said that marks on his body indicated that the boy had been kept bundled up in a tight space, possibly in the boot of a car. Dr Mant concluded that the cause of death was ligature strangulation. Roy's killer had wrapped a rope twice round the boy's neck and choked the life out of him. It was obvious, too, that he had been sexually assaulted. Police knew then that they had a vicious, sick killer on their hands – a homosexual child-killer.

The murder inquiry was headed by one of Scotland

Yard's most senior investigators, DS Percy Brown, and was later taken over by the Surrey Police.

A team of 40 detectives were drafted in from Scotland Yard and immediately formed their HQ at Leatherhead Police Station. At the weekends, this number was sometimes increased to 100 officers who spent their time making house-to-house enquiries. In addition, 12 more detectives set up an incident room at Kingston Police Station and a temporary police station was set up in a mobile caravan at the Bridge Road roundabout where Roy Tuthill was last seen. Large posters appealing to motorists were displayed at certain intervals along the A24 and further appeals for information were made in the press, radio and TV.

Over the next four months, 10,344 people were interviewed and over 2,000 written statements were taken. All males over the age of 14 near the estate where Roy was found, including residents of Brockham, Chessington and parts of Dorking, were asked to account for their movements on the days Roy went missing and was subsequently found.

The first-ever televised reconstruction of a crime was shown on TV in a bid to jog the memories of the viewers. Chief Inspector Doyle's 13-year-old son, Patrick, volunteered to dress up like the murdered boy and was filmed leaving Roy's school at 3.00pm and making his last known journey.

There was a specific inquiry into the sightings of the Austin Westminster car. In addition to detectives and officers from Surrey and Scotland Yard, detectives from Birmingham City Police took particulars of all the Austin Westminster cars ever manufactured at the company's

Longridge manufacturing plant. At Surrey County Council, detectives spent two weeks checking a million motor vehicle records at the council offices. In total, 1,800 owners of grey Austin Westminsters all over Britain were sought out and questioned – and eliminated from the inquiry. After four months of exhaustive investigations, the inquiry into Roy Tuthill's murder had not progressed.

The police were still convinced that the killer was a local man, though whether he continued to live locally after the murder remained questionable. Detectives considered he was most likely a secret pervert who hid his lust for young children from his closest domestic and business acquaintances. Perhaps he was an ostensibly happily married man with a job in the City and a home in the stockbroker belt of Surrey. He may possibly have a wife and they thought that perhaps his wife may hold the key to the killer's identity. They wondered whether she may have been away from home for a few days, so her husband seized his chance of touring the area, kerb-crawling in his car. Then he picked up a schoolboy, assaulted him, murdered him, then kept the body somewhere safe, perhaps in the boot of his own car. Perhaps his wife then returned home unexpectedly, and the killer panicked, particularly after the appeal appeared in the *Dorking Advertiser*, and realised he had to dump the body as soon as he possibly could.

And yet, for all the theories and investigations by the police, the outcome still remained 'murder by person or persons unknown', for a staggering total of 33 years. There were several reviews of the investigation and what little evidence there was over the decades following the murder. Indeed, the case became the only unsolved murder in the history of the county of Surrey.

The case seemed to have a slight breakthrough in 1983, when a middle-aged woman sent an anonymous letter to the *Dorking Advertiser* saying that she may have seen the Austin Westminster car. She had not come forward before, because she did not want to compromise a man she knew who dropped her off at the bus-stop on the A24 to Mickleham, on the day that Roy disappeared. While she stood at the bus-stop, she saw a silver-grey Austin Westminster turn up a steep, deeply rutted track towards the spot where the boy's body was found. She saw that car again over the coming months – perhaps eight or nine times. She described the driver as aged between 45 and 50 years old, wearing a narrow-brimmed trilby hat. However, she could not offer a name and did not leave contact details so the police could only add it to their list of witness statements and leave it at that.

Sir Peter Matthews, former Chief Constable of Surrey, was interviewed in the early 1980s by a local journalist. He said, 'The killer must have panicked and dumped the body, thinking, Any minute now someone will come along and I'll be caught – I must be quick. Why else would he make such little attempt to conceal the body? If he had taken it a few yards further on, to a more concealed spot, we would have taken ages to find it. I have pondered this case many, many times. God, it wasn't for lack of effort!'

Roy's family – his mother and father, sister and elder brother – moved away from Brockham soon after the murder. The fact that they were completely devastated goes without saying and they began to fall apart in private. In 1985, the head of Dorking CID, DI Richard Dunnford, told the press that 'the file is still open'. Indeed, unsolved cases, particularly murder cases, are never closed. It may be announced that the investigations have been officially called off, but the police still review the cases from time to time and renew their appeals through the media every few years, hoping that someone will cast their minds back to that time and something they had not realised before may suddenly occur to them.

In January 2001, a public review of the case was organised. A conference was held to discuss the unsolved murder and 25 detectives who had taken part in the original investigation – now retired and many in their seventies and eighties – were asked to come and support current investigating officers. The meeting was described by one officer as 'a case of the Sixties era of *Heartbeat* meeting with the 2001 era of *The Bill*'.

Former DCI Philip Doyle, 85 years old at the time, said of his return to the investigation, 'It's still fresh. I met Mr and Mrs Tuthill several times. What can you say about parents whose child has been murdered? They were two very sad people.'

DS David Cook, who was placed in charge of the reopened inquiry, said, 'The old former officers were incredibly helpful. They were the vital bridge between past and present. Their thoughts and memories proved a valuable tool in helping us understand what had taken place back then. Policing was all so different then and places have changed so dramatically in the intervening years.'

As he was featured in the press reviewing the case, Cook showed that he still had some of Roy's belongings, including the school books he was carrying on the day he was murdered.

Although the mood was optimistic, there were some

dissenters. With no new witness statements or tip-offs and a trail that had gone cold over 30 years previously, what chance had the investigating officers got of piecing together what really happened on that day and finding who had killed the schoolboy?

Little did they know it, though, they already had the answer within their grasp. A massively effective crime-fighting weapon which they did not have in the day of the murder was now available to them – the national DNA database. Now, whenever an arrest is made – even if the offender is not subsequently sent to prison, the police are quite within their rights to take a specimen of saliva which can then be analysed by the forensic lab and developed into a DNA profile – virtually unique to that person. A semen stain had been taken from the boy's trousers by the FSS and made into a DNA profile and this sample was stored under lock and key, along with other 'exhibits' salvaged from the crime scene. All it needed was for the killer to come to the attention of the police and there would be an instant match. They were completely unaware at this stage, though, that the answer to the murder was already logged on the database, dating from 1999, after a DNA sample from the killer had been added to it as a matter of routine.

The 65-year-old former gardener and farm worker, Brian Field, must have cursed himself. Had he not been over the legal limit as he climbed into his car after a drinking session at a pub in Sheldon, Birmingham, the elderly man would probably still be free. Driving down the road, he had passed a patrol car parked down a lane, and the officers in it must have considered him over the limit. The car veered erratically along the road, slightly clipping the kerb on one occasion, so he was pulled over and ordered to take a breathalyser test. When he failed the test, he was ordered to pay a £150 fine and a saliva sample was taken by the arresting officers and routinely added to the national database.

When the matched profile presented itself, murder detectives could not believe it. The review of the case had occurred only one month previously and the detectives, both old and new, were not expecting such a quick result, let alone any positive developments at all. Detectives were despatched to the man's house immediately. Arrested at his home on Wednesday, 21 February 2001, a police source said, 'Field had been very chatty with us. Then we asked him if he would mind giving some blood or hair for a DNA test. He didn't decide straight away and said he would sleep on it. The next morning, he said, "I have been telling you lies. I murdered Roy Tuthill."'

Three days later, on Saturday, 24 February 2001, Field was formally charged with the murder and a date was set for a trial at the Old Bailey. His first appearance was on 5 March. Colin Tuthill said, 'My prime reaction when I heard the case had been reopened and they had a suspect was surprise.'

Brian Field was born Brian Lull and brought up in a children's home with 12 other boys in Bourne, Lincolnshire, after he was abandoned by his mother, a prostitute, only a day after his birth, in 1936. He joined the choir and even took part in a BBC programme in 1951 with the home's owner and co-founder, and his foster father, Paul Field, on an edition of *This Is Your Life*. Paul Field was honoured by the Queen for his work in children's homes. A recent chairman of the Children's Family Trust was clearly shocked by the behaviour of a former Trust boy who turned into a paedophile and killer.

In 1959, Brian Field joined the Royal Marines, stationed in Malta and Cyprus for two years. On leaving, he worked as an engineer for the Milk Marketing Board, while living in Thames Ditton, Surrey. He was married twice and fathered three children, with his first wife, Celia, dying in a car crash in 1966 and his second wife, Mary, divorcing him after his many brushes with the law became public. He had an insatiable lust for sex with young boys and was apprehended on many occasions.

On the day of Roy's murder, Field had been drinking heavily. His wife was in hospital giving birth to their baby son, so Field took the opportunity to kerb-crawl the streets looking for a young victim. At about 4.00pm he got on to the Bridge Road roundabout and offered Roy Tuthill a lift in his white Mini – the exhaustive investigation into the Austin Westminster car had been a red herring despite the number of witnesses – and just minutes later, Colin, Roy's elder brother, went past on his scooter.

Field recounted how he pulled into a lay-by and forced Roy to remove his clothes and perform a sex act on him. He set off again but only to stop in another lay-by further on. It was there, Field told detectives, that he strangled Roy. The boy fought back, desperately attempting to remove the rope from around his neck, but he lost his fight for life. Field calmly told police, 'He just sort of convulsed a bit, sort of gasping for air and I just carried on and suddenly he went lifeless.'

Field put his body into the boot of the car and drove home. The most chilling aspect of the case was that he had parked his Mini in his driveway for three whole days with the body bundled up in a blanket in the boot the whole time, and returned home that day to see his wife and newborn baby son. As police searched for the 'local man', the killer was making plans to move home. Six weeks after the murder, they moved to Oswestry in Shropshire.

The following year, he was convicted of his first offence – attempting gross indecency – and was fined £20 by Wrexham magistrates. Three years later, Field was imprisoned after he attempted to abduct and assault a 14-year-old boy in Aberdeen. Although he was not questioned about Roy Tuthill's murder in the immediate investigation following the death, he was visited during this first term in prison, and was questioned about his possible involvement in the murder, but he denied all knowledge. Once out of prison, Field accepted the inevitable collapse of his marriage and he just continued as before. Further convictions followed for indecency in Oswestry and Shrewsbury, and he was given a four-year prison sentence for two counts of kidnap in Staffordshire.

Field had given a lift to two boys aged 14 and 16 and kept them in the car, where he threatened them and forced them to strip. Luckily, the lads escaped as the vehicle was moving and detectives believe that they could also have ended up as murder victims like Roy Tuthill had they not managed to escape. This had been his last prison term before his arrest in 2001.

Between his release from prison and his eventual arrest in 2001 for the murder of Roy Tuthill, Field moved to Solihull and worked as a gardener for cash, never paying tax or claiming benefits, and often working near children. When news of his arrest was made public, one shocked family told police, 'We trusted him and the children treated him as a kindly old uncle.' In fact, police only treated him as a suspect when one of his grown-up children discovered his criminal past and tipped off police that he was now residing in Solihull.

The trial was held at the Old Bailey on 5 March 2001. Judge Gerald Gordon described the killing as 'particularly obnoxious', saying, 'This was the killing of a normal, happy, healthy boy. These acts and their consequences must have haunted his parents for the rest of their lives and the family must still suffer. When you strangled him, I have no doubt that you sought to destroy the sole source of evidence against you. Thirty-three years later, you have been proved wrong.'

The judge warned that advances in scientific techniques 'should stand as a warning that there is no hiding place for sexual and violent criminals'.

Roy's aunt, Monique Gerin, said, 'Justice has been done at last. It is a shame that Roy's parents had to go to their graves not knowing that. After the murder, everyone went into their own personal grief, and communication between the family was lost. Christmases and so on were never the same again.'

His brother, Colin, paid tribute to the original murder squad led by DCS Philip Doyle. He said, 'I understand that one of the reasons they were able to pick up on the case now is because Mr Doyle did such an immaculate job with all the case papers and exhibits.'

Now retired, former DCS 'Paddy' Doyle said, 'I am so sorry for Roy's parents, Dennis and Hilary, who were not here to see this day. They were devastated by his death. Dennis died two years after the murder and Hilary in 1996.'

To her dying day, Roy's mother kept a picture of the lad

she never saw grow up by her bed. Her older son, Colin, told of how he still admits to feeling guilt that he couldn't protect his brother that day. He says, 'I don't know how it affected Dad because he kept expressions inside. At the time of Roy's death, Mother was very weepy. For the rest of her life, there was a photo of Roy beside her bed. It was like a shrine. The first years or so I wanted revenge. But things evolve and that emotion is not there any more. I always imagined that, if it had not been solved in the early stages, it was never going to be solved. But I'm grateful to the police for never giving up.'

One of his victims, now grown up, said of Field, 'He was an athlete – an impressive man who loved cricket, football and rugby. But he had a way of talking that was almost effeminate. It was an era, too, when you didn't complain about what he did to you or what he asked you to do to him. He was evil personified. He was a very dangerous man who was consumed by lust.'

The current case officer, DCS David Cook, said that Field now looked like 'an elderly, frail man. That is the image – but, as we came to know, he was a dangerous man who could integrate himself into people's lives. Appearances can be deceptive. He is not just a child murderer but also a convicted paedophile. It gives me a sense of relief to know that Field will surely die in prison.'

Although he has been convicted on more than one occasion on charges of indecency and kidnap – some of which may have resulted in murder had the intended victims not managed to escape – is Field just guilty of the one murder? Police believe it to be inconceivable that such a devious, violent man is only responsible for the crimes of which he was convicted.

Since Field's conviction, detectives have been tracing men and women who say they were sexually abused by him as youngsters, though few wished to give evidence against him at a trial after so long. Police forces nationwide, led by Surrey Police, are to review at least 25 cases of child murder or mysterious disappearances that are suspected to have ended in murder. The first eight cases are viewed as the core of the review, being the cases most likely to have been committed by Field. Although he admitted to the murder of Roy Tuthill, detectives realise that this was only after they asked him for a DNA sample whereupon he realised he was to be convicted whatever his answer. But with the absence of any DNA samples saved from other crime scenes – particularly disappearances, rather than definite murders – they may be solely reliant on Field's willingness to help – and, so far, he has shown none. A special conference held among police forces across the UK has been held to discuss the whereabouts of Brian Field in relation to other unsolved crimes. DI Chuck Burton, who runs a national register of child murders and sexual assaults, said Field was one of the most dangerous offenders he had ever met.

Among the unsolved sex crimes and disappearances due to be reviewed include the death of 15-year-old Mark Billington, who was found dead hanging from a tree in a wooded area off the A45 in Meriden, near Solihull – where Field lived – in 1984. The death was considered to be suicide, but his parents always maintained it was murder. He set off from home on his bicycle which was never found and his body was only discovered two months after he went missing. After Field was convicted,

Mark's father, Roy, told the BBC, 'We have said all along that someone befriended him, then abducted and subsequently murdered him.'

The other case files include the disappearance of two friends on Boxing Day 1996. Thirteen-year-old David Spencer and 11-year-old Patrick Warren were last seen playing in Chelmsley Wood, near Solihull. Despite pleas from their families, the two boys were never seen again. Police thought they had run away at the time, but now their disappearances are being re-examined. After all, why would two otherwise healthy, happy young boys run away from home, leaving behind their Christmas presents, including a new bicycle, the day after they received them?

Surrey Police issued a statement on their website on 15 November 2001, reviewing their investigation of the case. Commenting on the investigation, DCS Cook, said, 'I find myself in a very rewarding position in that I was able to bring this matter to a successful conclusion. This case was solved on 23 April 1968 thanks to the professionalism of the officers involved in the original and subsequent investigations. In 1968, who could have foreseen the advances in both investigative techniques and forensic science, which have both clearly contributed to the success today?

'Brian Lunn Field is, and will remain, an extremely dangerous man. His conviction today will clearly make the United Kingdom a much safer place. He has admitted his guilt, but the investigation into his activities will go on to determine the full extent of his criminal past. Through his own admission of guilt, he is a dangerous man. I therefore appeal to any person who has information about his criminal past to come forward in order that other possible victims of his activities may also see justice done.'

It was in December 2000 that the National Crime Faculty identified Brian Lunn Field as a possible suspect after comparative case analysis of abduction offences at various locations across the UK. As a result, he was scheduled to be one of the first people from whom DNA would be sought, in order to confirm his involvement in other cases.

Mr Jonathan Smith, the specialist adviser who co-ordinated the work on the Roy Tuthill case by the FSS, said, 'Forensic scientists have provided support to the inquiry into the death of Roy Tuthill since 1968. During this time, changes in the way the FSS handles forensic casework, as well as the advent of sensitive DNA testing techniques, means the FSS has been able to provide results to the police and help them with one of the older, unsolved cases.'

8

96 HOURS OF CARNAGE

One of the qualifying features of a serial killer is that his murder count must be at least three or above, where each of the slayings is carried out as a separate act but for the same basic reasons. Philip John Smith qualified for the title in just 96 hours, going from zero to three in record time.

Philip Smith did not share some of the common serial killer characteristics – he was not a known offender and was not known to have hurt animals or other humans, and so had, apparently, turned to his task quite late in his life. However, when the master switch was thrown, Smith adopted the role of serial killer with great relish.

An unemployed joiner, handyman and fairground worker, Smith kept an occasional job at his local pub, The Rainbow, in the Digbeth area of Birmingham. It was from these premises that he also earned some extra money as an unlicensed taxi driver. He was known by many of the locals, trusted in the main and had given no one any cause for concern.

On 9 November 2000, the course of Smith's life underwent a sudden and dramatic change when he committed his first murder, for reasons that are still not known today. The clock was now ticking and further mayhem would follow.

Two officers patrolling a recreation ground off Golden Hillock Road in the Sparkbrook area of Birmingham made a gruesome discovery, when they noticed what looked like the smouldering remains of a fire. On closer inspection, they could see that the pile of rags on the floor was, in fact, the wrapped-up remains of a body. The finding was reported to the station and the scene was sealed off ready for the arrival of the FSS team who would comb the entire area looking to locate the smallest traces of forensic material that could give the police a clue, in what was undoubtedly a murder, and in which the murderer had also attempted to destroy the evidence.

The body was eventually identified as that of 21-year-old Jodie Hyde, a recovering butane gas addict. A post-mortem examination, which identified her through fingerprints, showed that she had died of strangulation, before being rolled up in a blanket, tied with green rope and set on fire. She was naked and had suffered 60 per cent burns to her body, destroying much of the available evidence and making identification of the victim by normal means a most difficult task.

A few days later, on 12 November, the landlord of the Robin Hood public house at Rashwood, near Droitwich Spa, Worcestershire, discovered the body of another lady in a wooded lane on the perimeter of a garden adjoining a nursing home.

After the police had arrived, the location was, once again, sealed off and FSS scientists meticulously scoured the site for evidence. On post-mortem examination, the body was identified through dental records as being that of 25-year-old mother of three Rosemary Corcoran. She had suffered such a severe battering that she was physically unrecognisable, her face being entirely shattered. She was so badly disfigured that her dental records were the only way of making a positive identification and, in order to complete this procedure, the pathologist had first to reconstruct the jaw. The police were now considering the possibility of the attacks being linked, while at the same time maintaining two distinct murder inquiries. However, they would not have to wait too long to receive more news that would convince them that they were indeed looking for one perpetrator.

Only hours later on the same day, just 20 miles away in Lea Bank, Birmingham, a dog-walker found the battered body of 39-year-old mother of six, Carol Jordan, in parkland often used by members of the public. She had also been viciously beaten and, again, her identity was confirmed only through the use of dental records.

Although the cases were clearly different, with no standard modus operandi, the police were now convinced that the murderer was just one person, although they were taken aback at the speed with which the body count was climbing. They had gone from one murder to three in just four days, two obviously occurring within hours of each other. The West Midlands Police Force and their colleagues from neighbouring West Mercia Police now believed they were dealing with a particularly brutal serial killer, whose workrate was so high that the need to apprehend him was paramount if they were not to end up facing a regional massacre. The forces now brought the full might of their investigating powers to bear on the case, applying more than 100 detectives and a further 50 support staff to the task of tracking down the assailant. Codenamed Operation Green, it was led by the Chief Constable of West Midlands Police, Sir Edward Crew.

In addition to the manpower provided by the local forces, the FSS now applied specific staff members to provide expert scientific support. Two members of staff – one a senior forensic-scene examiner and the other a DNA expert – attended the crime scenes and also attended the post-mortems to advise on, among other things, the collection of samples.

The police investigation began in earnest. Every detail of the victims' lives was looked at in a bid to find some strand that would link them to the killer. The police wanted to know where they worked, who they lived with, their family connections, friendships and their general social environment and, importantly, their exact movements on the day of their deaths and on the days leading up to it. The investigation was a time-consuming process, with each detail being collected, logged and cross-checked. All those who knew the victims had to be tracked down, through family, friends and work colleagues, in order to get a clear picture of the lives of each of them.

After a while, a number of coincidental facts emerged that begged closer inspection. Each of the victims frequented The Rainbow pub in the Digbeth area of Birmingham. Just coincidence maybe, but this also meant that the victims either knew each other, or at least unwittingly may have been in each other's company there. It may, on the other hand, have meant that they knew the same group of people, and it is facts like these that the police wished to explore further.

Visiting the pub, they asked the landlord and regulars questions about the victims. It was at this point that Philip Smith first came to the attention of the police. He said he knew of the women concerned and had befriended both Jodie and Rosemary in the months before they were killed. Beyond this, the police received no further information that would help open the case up. Those questioned during the investigation were themselves scrutinised, but found to be of generally good character. Philip Smith, of course, had no previous criminal history, no tendency even to small-scale violence. Although obviously a big man, a man capable of inflicting the type of horrific injuries the victims suffered, he was at that time beyond suspicion.

The police now knew that the victims had all been in the same area over a period of time and now called for all CCTV footage recorded in and around the district at that time to be made available to them. These cameras stationed all over most city centres would passively watch and capture the public's movements, occasionally recording for posterity people's less attractive behaviour. It just might have been possible for the police to locate one or more of the victims, possibly in the company of someone they had not yet interviewed.

Hours and hours of footage was reviewed before the police were finally rewarded with a scene that would give them another line of enquiry. There on screen, captured for all to see, was Philip Smith, struggling with Rosemary Corcoran outside a club in Handsworth. The CCTV date and time code showed that the event occurred just hours before Rosemary's body was found. If he wasn't the killer, he was one of the last people who knew her to have seen her alive.

The police moved in fast and arrested Smith on suspicion of the murder of Rosemary Corcoran. A warrant was issued to search Smith's dingy terraced home in Braithwaite Road in the Sparkbrook area of Birmingham, while he was held in custody and interviewed regarding his relationship with the victim, and was asked to account for his movements after they had left the club. Smith denied any involvement in Rosemary's murder and suggested that they had gone to the club separately and had met there by chance. They had a minor disagreement on leaving the club and had argued outside. He had then gone home and she had set off alone to make her own way home. He did not see her again and had not volunteered this information during his initial interview for fear of becoming involved in the murder inquiry.

As Smith continued to deny any involvement in the second murder, the police now tried to establish his movements around the time of the other murders and, once again, Smith provided himself with alibis, yet seemed unable to provide the names of witnesses who would be able to corroborate his claims. The police were now quite suspicious of Smith and waited apprehensively for the outcome of the detailed search of his home.

Meanwhile, an appeal for information from the public turned up a pensioner, who said he saw a man who fitted Smith's description, with apparent bloodstains on his trousers, filling a petrol can in Bromsgrove, a neighbouring town to Droitwich. This was just a few hours after the moment when Smith was caught on CCTV arguing with Rosemary Corcoran.

The circumstantial evidence was now building and the police were now more inclined than ever to think that the man they had in custody was the multiple killer they were looking for. Smith, however, was not ready to agree and continued to deny any involvement, remaining adamant that nothing that the police had shown up to that point proved that he had killed anyone. Yes, he had argued with Rosemary, but he hadn't killed her. As for the pensioner's statement, it was a coincidental likeness, but not him.

Unfortunately, the garage that served the petrol on that evening had not got any video footage and the staff could not remember specifically anything about the man who had filled the petrol can.

Meanwhile, FSS scientists were carefully examining Smith's flat in Braithwaite Road, Sparkbrook, just a few blocks from where Jodie Hyde's body was found, and they were also checking his Volvo car. On entering the dingy flat, the forensic scientists were drawn immediately to the scene in the bathroom, where floating in a bath of murky-brown water appeared to be a number of bloodstained items of clothing. Yet this was only the beginning; the FSS team now examined each room in minute detail, and each and every item to be found in them.

The results were to provide a massive body of evidence that would point conclusively to the guilt of Philip Smith as the mass murderer. Analysis of the clothes in the bath eventually established that they had been worn by Miss Corcoran on the night she was killed. The link was further supported by a forensic examination of the trousers which proved that semen extracted from the gusset of the garment belonged to Miss Corcoran's boyfriend, Mark Sultan. Also found soaking in the bath were a pair of 44in-waist jeans belonging to Smith. Examination of the jeans revealed bloodstains of two types, one belonging to Miss Corcoran and the other matching the blood of Carol Jordan. Another substance also found on the jeans could have come from Jodie Hyde, although this link was less dependable.

The FSS team also found a pair of steel-toe-capped boots on which were found traces of blood matching both Mrs Jordan and Miss Corcoran. And, as has been documented, the chance of the blood not coming from the victims was considered to be a billion to one. The evidence was becoming overwhelming.

A stick found in the bathroom, possibly used for stirring the bath and pushing the clothes around, was also found to have traces of blood on the end that matched that of Jodie Hyde.

Tiny pink fibres were also found at Smith's address and in his car, which matched the fibres of the blanket which had been wrapped around Miss Hyde's body when she was burned.

Just outside the front door of Smith's flat, the investigators found a carrier bag containing further damning evidence. The bag was stuffed with pill bottles from Mark's Chemist, including Jodie Hyde's methadone prescription collected on the day she disappeared, lighter fuel, which she was known to sniff, and her birth certificate.

Smith's car was to provide a range of further evidence

that would give the police all they would need to make a formal charge. On closer inspection, the FSS team were able to isolate traces of Miss Corcoran's blood on both the offside tyre and the mud flap. The same blood type was also detected on the rear offside wing. On the inside of the car, bloodstains located on the back of the front passenger headrest were identified as having come from Jodie Hyde. A bloody fingerprint found on the rear window was shown to have a partial match to that of Miss Corcoran.

Impressions were taken of the tyres and were matched exactly to those found at the scene where Miss Corcoran's body was found. The same tread pattern was also partially matched to impressions taken from the inside of Miss Corcoran's arm, inflicted when she was hit by Smith's car. Clearly, the tread patterns found on the tyres of Smith's car would match many vehicles. Taken in isolation, this piece of evidence would be circumstantial and would not have the weight to provide a conviction. However, considered among all of the other evidence, it would be another firm nail in Smith's coffin. More persuasive evidence was found when a piece of coloured indicator lens, which had been found at the scene of Rosemary Corcoran's murder, matched the shape missing from a broken indicator lens on Smith's car.

Further examination of Mr Jordan's trousers showed traces of paint which matched the paint from Smith's car, again, by itself, not proof beyond doubt, but taken as a piece of the overall jigsaw it added another significant factor which any juror would find difficult to put down to coincidence.

In December 2000, the police team formally charged Philip John Smith with the murders of Jodie Hyde,

Rosemary Corcoran and Carol Jordan and he would be held in police custody until the case could be brought to court. Once charged, Smith continued to deny any involvement in the murders and seemed to disregard entirely the weight of evidence against him.

The trial opened on Tuesday, 3 July 2001, at Leicester Crown Court, Mrs Justice Rafferty presiding. Having been read the charges, Smith pleaded not guilty and the prosecution then took the floor. Prosecuting lawyer Timothy Raggatt told the assembled jurors that Smith had strangled and set fire to his first victim, beat and drove over the second and clubbed the third to death. The second victim, Rosemary Corcoran, had been taken from a Birmingham nightclub on Remembrance Sunday to the Rashwood area of Birmingham, where Smith pulled her from the car, beat her, stripped her and drove over her.

Those who found the bodies were called as witnesses as the prosecution outlined the scene of each crime, before they started to present the evidence that would conclusively link Smith to the murders.

Once the court heard how bloodstains from the victims had been found at his flat, on his clothes and in and on his car, Smith was asked to explain how this had come about. In a final bid to wriggle free from the jaws of justice, Smith claimed that, for some reason, the police had planted the evidence in an attempt to frame someone for the murders. Defence counsel Rachael Brand QC asked Mr Smith if he had formed any idea as to how blood, said to have come from the victims, had been found on his jeans. Mr Smith replied, 'The police may have tampered with it or something like that.' He then gave the same explanation when asked why the blood of Miss Corcoran and Mr Jordan had been found on his steel-toe-capped boots. The court then heard how a pair of size-ten women's trousers, which the prosecution claimed belonged to Miss Corcoran, were found soaking in Mr Smith's bath. His response was that the trousers were among clothes he had stolen from outside an Oxfam shop in the middle of the night. Why other garments were not singled out to be washed that night remained unanswered. He told the court, 'There are bags that are left outside shops that I pick up and take back to my flat at night-time.'

As the prosecution continued to reveal evidence against Smith, the outcome appeared to be beyond doubt. After days of wrangling, Smith's defence lawyer told the judge that Smith had indicated to her that he wanted to change his plea and would like to have the charges re-read to him. And so, 11 days into the trial, the clerk of the court read out again the charges against Smith and, on each occurrence, he answered, 'Guilty', prompting tears from relatives of the victims, who were watching the proceedings from the public gallery.

James Taylor, Carol Jordan's brother, said afterwards, 'The devastation and the heartache that Philip Smith has caused will never fade. The last eight months have been a nightmare for all of us, especially Carol's husband and children. The past is now over but not forgotten. We are all hoping that Philip Smith will never – and I mean never – be allowed into the outside world ever again.

Sentencing Smith to life imprisonment, Mrs Justice Rafferty said, 'You robbed three innocent ladies of their lives. I suspect that their families will suffer more as they simply don't understand why you did it. The brutality of these ladies' deaths, designed by you to evade discovery, showing the coldness with which you despatched them, is appalling. You should clearly have faced up like a man at the overwhelming nature of the Crown's case against you but you chose to put the victims' families through misery which you compounded by this trial.'

Speaking after the trial, senior forensic scientist Martin Whittaker, who co-ordinated the case for the FSS, said, 'A team of forensic scientists from a number of different specialities worked really hard to gather everything they could. The team pulled together every strand of forensic evidence to create a kind of "spider's web" and, in the centre of it all, linked to each one of the murdered women, was Philip Smith. This was a difficult case to deal with because there was so much evidence to look at. In 20 years of working for the FSS, I have never had to deal with so much in relation to one suspect ... it was quite overwhelming. The results of our work gave the police a very strong case against Smith. Throughout the investigation, the FSS and the police worked very closely together and the result is a tribute to that partnership.

'I would like to record my thanks to all those involved in the inquiry and hope that its success in putting an evil and dangerous man behind bars for life will bring some comfort to the victims' families.'

Following the successful prosecution of Smith, the police began to look back at other unsolved murders, disappearances and suspicious deaths. West Midlands Police Chief Superintendent Ellie Baker said, 'Philip Smith is already a triple killer and we would be wrong to leave it at that ... we need to search further.'

Police from six forces then held a secret meeting to

determine whether up to 40 unsolved murders could be linked to Smith. Nine specifically had been compiled by the National Crime Faculty at Bramshill in Hampshire. Chief Superintendent Ellie Baker then chaired a meeting of the heads of CID from six forces, which was held at Hindlip Hall, the headquarters of West Mercia Police. At the meeting, each force gave a briefing on past murders in their region and then they were asked to go away and study the results of the West Midlands Police investigation into Smith's known murders.

Out of that joint meeting came suspicions that Smith could have murdered Patricia Lynott, a barmaid who had worked at The Rainbow pub, where Smith had previously been employed, and a place where each of his victims had been a customer.

Patricia Lynott's body was found in her flat in Bordersley Green, Birmingham, just 14 days before Smith strangled Jodie Hyde. At the time, it was thought that Mrs Lynott had died of natural causes; despite the inconclusive outcome of the post-mortem, her body had been released for burial and she was taken back to her home town of Athlone in the Irish Republic.

Mrs Lynott's daughter, Anna, had said that she had spoken with her mother on the phone on 17 October 2000. A neighbour had spotted Mrs Lynott entering her flat carrying shopping on the same day. Her body was found on her bedroom floor six days later.

It was known that, occasionally, Smith would give Mrs Lynott a lift home. On one occasion, he had put his arm across her front door, barring her entry. Although she had felt trapped and frightened, she had managed to gain entry, and subsequently reported the incident to her boss at The Rainbow, who confronted Smith with the claim.

With a growing suspicion, the West Midlands Police requested that the body of Patricia Lynott be exhumed for further pathological analysis, and obtained a court order to do so. Her remains were taken to a Dublin mortuary where three British pathologists and the Irish State pathologist carried out a detailed post-mortem. At the previous post-mortem, the pathologist had noticed bruising consistent with an assault or a fall, but had concluded that this could not have been the cause of death. Her larynx had not been fractured and so they were able to conclude that she had not been strangled.

Unfortunately, after much extensive post-mortem investigation, the pathologists were unable to provide any additional information and so the body was once again buried with a low-key church service.

The police continue to check the details of other murders, with one police insider observing that 'there is a strong suspicion among officers that Smith is indeed responsible for other crimes and we are hopeful of uncovering these in due course'.

Meanwhile, the motives for Smith's crimes remain unknown. Following his incarceration, he has remained tight-lipped about the nature of his known crimes and is not indicating any involvement in any others. Due to the savagery of his crimes and the multiple nature of them, it is unlikely that Smith will ever win parole and so could only help his cause by being as helpful as possible. But, like many serial killers before him, he may take the details of his criminal life with him to the grave.

Psychologists seeking to attribute Smith's killing spree to some factor have struggled to come up with anything that adequately explains his actions. One factor, though, is believed to be the lack of a permanent sexual relationship, a feature considered by many to be the driving force behind many of the world's serial murderers.

For now, we do not know Smith's true reasons and probably never will but, more than ever, with the growing skills of scientists from the FSS, we can expect eventually to track these people down and bring them to justice.

9

MURDER FOR MONEY

The police officer shook his head. Only a fortnight into the New Year and the calls from elderly people claiming to have been burgled just kept coming.

He felt sorry for lonely pensioners living alone, with no one to talk to and precious little to occupy them, making up excuses to get a visit from the police for a bit of company. Not much different from hypochondriacs who visit doctors with imagined symptoms, he thought.

Miss Jean Barnes stood in the hall waiting for the officer as he descended the stairs. The man shook his head. 'I'm sorry, madam. No signs of forced entry. Nothing missing.'

'I tell you, young man, I'm being burgled. I know this house and its contents like the back of my hand and my antiques are going missing.'

As she watched the police officer disappear down the driveway, Miss Barnes knew what they thought – that she was a silly old lady making up stories for a bit of company. With family and friends paying her regular visits, Jean Barnes had no need of further company and was far from lonely. She was no senile old bat. A former interpreter and translator for the Civil Service, who spoke six languages fluently, she had been one of the first women ever to graduate from Cambridge University. And they thought she was losing it!

She would telephone Sussex Police the next day to report the officer's behaviour. Her valuable antique collection, amassed over many years, was being plundered piece by piece, week by week, and she was having none of it.

Later that month, she would call the police to report another burglary, then again to claim she had been attacked on her doorstep by an intruder, by which time the police had notified the Social Services, suggesting that she might benefit from social calls from carers. A Crime Prevention Officer paid her a visit that February, replacing all the doors and windows in her home to give her more security and peace of mind.

Months later, however, Jean Barnes would claim she had received bogus phone calls from someone demanding to know her personal bank details, although these claims were all taken with a pinch of salt.

On 26 July 1999, WPC Sarah Loveland arrived at the large 13-room semi-detached house on Tennyson Road. A report that Jean Barnes, an elderly spinster who lived there alone, had not been seen or heard of for several days resulted in the officer being despatched to her home.

She knocked on the front door but received no reply and so checked for an unlocked door or window through which she could gain entry. After finding the front and back doors securely locked, she broke the glass of a rear window and climbed in. Searching the house from top to bottom, she saw Miss Barnes lying in the centre of a cluttered room.

It was immediately obvious that she was dead and, judging from the odour, had been dead for quite some time. Her decomposing corpse was partly hidden under a blanket and her dressing gown forced over her head, indicating that someone had been present after her death to cover her up. WPC Loveland removed the blanket to make a closer examination. She observed that the pensioner had suffered a serious head injury and then, later, discovered blood in the hallway.

Her blind neighbour, Hilda Woolven, had become worried as she had not seen her friend for several days, so she had called the police earlier that day. She later told them, 'Jean was very security conscious. When I was there, we would rarely answer her door to anyone. I don't know of any reason why anyone would want to harm her in any way.'

The subsequent post-mortem showed that Miss Barnes had been hit on the head with a heavy object with at least one sharp edge. The various wounds on her arms and body showed that she had tried to defend herself from the heavy blows aimed at her by the killer.

Sussex Police launched a murder inquiry by tracing Miss Barnes's antiques through dealers around the UK and abroad, including Christie's and Sotheby's. Eventually, the trail led straight back to various antique shops in Worthing.

Meanwhile, the police urgently needed some idea of the

type of person who had committed the crime. Dr Julian Boon, psychology lecturer at Leicester University, had acted as a criminal profiler on many investigations and was glad to help police with this inquiry.

The case itself was confusing; an old lady lies battered to death in her own home, many of her possessions are found to be missing and there's no sign of a break-in or motive or murder weapon.

Following the murder, Dr Boon worked with police every step of the way. Initial checks into her financial background revealed that she had property worth over £500,000. Police recalled that, months before her death, she had reported a burglary to them. She had also reported bogus phone calls concerning her bank account details. By carefully examining the way her body was positioned and how she died, Dr Boon told police, 'It seemed pre-planned, which made me think it could be a regular visitor to the house – and who lived very close to the victim. I was sure the killer's motive was theft and they probably had a history of fraud and deception.'

It was not clear as to the exact date and time of the 87-year-old's death, which hampered the pursuit of clear witness accounts and potential suspects, but Boon immediately suspected that the killer had been highly clinical in his approach to the murder. He surmised that the killer was neither a sadist nor a paranoid schizophrenic, but a calculating man who murdered in cold blood; a man to whom murder was merely a necessary evil, and an occupational hazard which comes with the task of theft. Boon directed DS Steve Scott and his murder squad towards a killer who committed murder for money.

A police appeal through TV and the national media led to several suspects being sought for questioning. Other suspects included two local milkmen, John and Johnny Gosling, father and son, who worked the Tennyson Road milk round. At the time of the murder, they both worked out of the Co-Op's depot in Worthing. On the day the body was discovered, 2 July 1999, the father had covered the round for his son who had overslept. John Gosling left a pint of milk and found a note intended for his son. His son said he was surprised that she had asked for an extra wholemeal loaf because she only had one loaf a week and the last one had only been on the previous Friday. His son, Johnny, took over the round and, on the Friday, he left a pint of milk and inside Miss Barnes's bread-bin was a cheque for £6.30.

On 29 September, John and Johnny Gosling were both arrested. The 49-year-old father and former Royal Marine was arrested in front of colleagues at the dairy and taken to Bognor Police Station for questioning, while his 26-year-old son,. Johnny, was arrested at his home in Southwick and taken to Crawley Police Station. While they were both being questioned, police officers searched their homes for anything which might incriminate them.

John Gosling Sr said, 'I kept turning things over in my mind. I knew I had done nothing wrong but I started to believe I was going to be charged with murder. My solicitor kept telling them they had no evidence to justify holding either one of us and, as it was, the police were currently committing unlawful arrest. After 36 hours they released us on police bail with the understanding that we had to make ourselves available for questioning again.'

During the subsequent court case, his son told defence

counsel Christopher Kinch, 'As far as I was concerned, I had done nothing wrong. I had given the police all the help I could.' He described how he and his father's clothing had been taken away and analysed. The police told them they wanted to test it for DNA samples. He said, 'The thrust of it was that they suspected me of being responsible for Miss Barnes's death.' He said that his father had also been arrested on suspicion of the murder having been the result of a 'two-man job'. He was kept in custody overnight, before they released him but he was served with a witness summons to appear in court, even though he didn't want to bring it all up again.

It was the younger of the two men who had first alerted police to a handwritten note, apparently from Miss Barnes. It read, 'Dear Milkman, I am so sorry but I am going into Hospital on Monday, 24 July. Then I will be going into a Nursing Home. Therefore could you please leave me the Bill on Friday, 23 July and a loaf today, Thankyou for your kindness, (signed) JA Barnes, 9 Tennyson Road, Worthing.'

Mr Gosling Jr said, 'I had not noticed if it was in her handwriting because that is not the sort of thing that you pay attention to at three o'clock in the morning. I remember screwing it up and throwing it away in the rubbish box in the milk van. However, as I hardly ever need to empty it, it was still there some time after and I handed it over to the police.'

His father said, 'Neither of us had ever even met Miss Barnes. She was on Johnny's round but she used to leave a note and a cheque once a fortnight to pay for her milk. That is the only contact we had with her.'

The case was featured on the BBC's *Crimewatch*

programme in 1998. Several weeks later, the case was featured again and it included the forged note to the milkman, and the letter itself jogged the memory of one viewer.

Mrs Audrey Ridpath recognised the handwriting as that belonging to David Munley, an odd-job man who had done some decorating jobs for her and her neighbour in the past. Four years previously, Miss Barnes and her neighbour, Mrs Winifred Smith, had almost been conned out of money when Munley stole cheques from them while decorating their homes, forged their signatures and attempted to cash them in their names to the tune of £5,000 but, when confronted with the evidence, he had admitted his guilt and handed back the money. As the money had been recovered, neither woman reported him to the police.

Based on Mrs Ridpath's recollections, Boon looked at what little they knew about David Munley and it was his ideas which led Scott and his team to concentrate their investigations on this particular individual. Had it not been for Mrs Ridpath, Munley would probably never have come to the attention of the police as he had no previous convictions, though he did fit the offender profile exactly: a middle-aged man who lived very close to the victim – just 400 yards away from Tennyson Road on Byron Road, Worthing – who had lied to his wife, stolen from the elderly before and had little or no capacity for conscience.

Julian Boon advised Scott on a low-key arrest with one police car and no sirens. The detective planned to delay the arrest because it happened to be David Munley's birthday, but Boon pointed out that there was no need.

This man, he assured Scott, would have no emotional or sentimental attachments to any type of anniversary. The killer of Miss Barnes had a one-track mind, a single pursuit of money and success; simply, that 'he will have one aim and one aim only – that is how not to get caught for it'.

During the subsequent interrogation, Munley behaved exactly as Boon predicted he would. Scott presented him with the forged note to the milkman and the matched handwriting indentified by Audrey Ridpath, to which Munley promptly clammed up 'like Blair at question time'.

Soon, the team had amassed overwhelming evidence against Munley, including a whole host of forensic clues, so he was formally arrested and a date for the trial was arranged.

The trial started on Tuesday, 14 November 2000, and was expected to last four weeks. David Munley wore a grey suit and open-necked shirt. He stood accused of one count of murder, nine counts of burglary and five counts of forgery.

At the trial, the prosecution claimed that David Munley had broken into the victim's home and must have thought his luck was in when he discovered her virtual Aladdin's Cave of treasures. Over the coming months, with a failed marriage and business behind him, and fuelled by greed, Munley saw the antiques and thought of cash. He returned over and over again to steal from Miss Barnes, with the temptation to continue the serial burglary being just too great to resist. As one visit led to another, he was caught by the owner, turning the greedy burglar into a killer.

Mr Jeremy Gompertz QC, for the prosecution, said, 'On some occasion in the middle of July, he was seen in the house by Miss Barnes who confronted him, perhaps, and it was then that he battered her about the head until she died.'

Even after the murder, he couldn't help returning to plunder even more antiques. On visits following the murder, he used a dressing gown and blanket to cover his victim, so that he did not have to look at her, and continued to empty Miss Barnes's home of her worldly possessions. In addition, several documents belonging to Miss Barnes had been found under floorboards at David Munley's home, and his phone bill revealed he had made several calls to Miss Barnes's home telephone, indicating that his victim really had been the receiver of several bogus calls from someone attempting to further plunder her bank account.

Again, Boon was proved correct. Even though there was damning evidence against him, he forced his lawyers to refute all of the evidence, loudly proclaiming his innocence. In court, he came across as cocky and confident, laughing out loud at the case for the prosecution, even though, under the surface, a desperate man was hiding. He was, as Boon predicted he would, 'going for broke. There must be a way that he thinks he'll win.'

On Friday, 1 December 2000, David Munley gave evidence for the first time. Questioned about the antiques he had sold, he said he had bought them off friends and from car-boot sales, and claimed to have no recollection of several items such as paintings, a clock and china which the prosecution argued had come from the house. He admitted selling the rest, but said that he'd bought other items after he'd won a £700 double-win at horse-racing and went to purchase them at car-boot sales, antique fairs and charity shops. He said he had been buying and selling antiques since his company Fire Safety UK Ltd went into liquidation several years ago.

He said, 'Both my former wife Judith and I had an interest in nice things and used to go round charity shops to try and build up a few things and sell them on. I remember buying two paintings at an antique fair on Lancing Green. I can remember a lady gave one to me in exchange for papering and decorating her hallway, because she didn't have any cash.'

Several other items, including a Davenport desk and an orrery (a model of the planetary system), came from a Mrs Roderick, and an unnamed resident of Church Walk, Worthing. Police did house-to-house enquiries, asking about the two residents. DC Patrick Payne said, 'No one had ever heard of them, including some residents who had lived there for more than 20 years.'

Munley claimed that silverware and other items which he pawned came from his ex-wife. He said, 'They were definitely Judith's. The teapot has always been special to her because it was something to do with her mother.' And Judith Munley, who divorced him in 1985, told the jury that a silver teapot, a holder for a soda siphon, a decanter and a scent bottle, had all belonged to her.

Munley sold some of the goods to Acorn Antiques of Worthing, where he was known only as 'Geordie'. Joint owner of the shop Peter Nichols told the court how Munley claimed the antiques came from his aunt's house in Sussex. He said, 'She had left the contents to him and his brother with the money going into a trust and the house had been left to the church.' He said that Munley had told him that he and his brother had been clearing the house and bringing it down to a lock-up in Littlehampton. Munley had also chatted to Mr Nichols about his trips to Thailand, where he claimed he had a girlfriend and where he owned land. Mr Nichols even visited Munley at his flat to look at some antiques. He described Munley's home as a messy bachelor's flat which he shared with his Jack Russell.

Frank Wilson of Wilson Antiques, also in Worthing, told the court that he paid Munley £500 for an antique clock, 11 days before the victim's body was found. Mr Wilson said, 'When Munley brought the clock, he was happy to supply proof of his identity and gave me no reason to be suspicious. I was happy that the piece was his to sell from the questions I asked, his general appearance and the way he talked about the piece.'

Andrew Wilson (no relation) of Heptinstall Jewellers, Worthing, bought and pawned several antiques from Munley in July 1999. He paid Munley £1,750 for an ornate clock and orrery which Munley sold to him. Other pawned items included a decanter, silver-plated teapot and dish-holder. He said, 'I seem to remember he said he was clearing a house for an aunt or something like that.'

Police questioned Mr Jeremy Winn, the nephew of Miss Barnes, and he said he could identify several pieces stolen from her, which had been retraced through various auction houses, including furniture, pictures, china pots and a tea set. He described how several of the antiques had triggered memories from his childhood, and said he was certain these were the same pieces. He last visited his aunt's house a full 12 years before her death in 1999, and remembered that the house was untidy and dusty and that his aunt had been mainly living on the first floor of the house. He added that the position of the furniture appeared to have changed little over the years, and he thought he would have noticed if any of the items had gone missing by then.

John Birkett, a forensic scientist, said that none of Munley's fingerprints had been found in the house. Given that no one had seen him going in or out, how he actually broke into the house remains unknown. The police had scoured Miss Barnes's home for footprints after the discovery of her body. He said that footprints left by police at the crime scene had been eliminated from the investigation and unknown prints were found on the kitchen lino. 'Some of the marks on the lino had the same pattern as Mr Munley's shoes. There were no obvious marks that corresponded to other pairs of shoes. There were many other marks on the lino and they were eliminated against other items of footwear. There is strong support for the suggestion that the marks on the floor-covering had been made by Mr Munley's shoes.'

However, the case was not watertight. Under cross-examination by the defence, Mr Birkett admitted, 'There could be a shoe somewhere that would give a similar match.' He also agreed that two other unidentified footprints had been found.

However, more forensic evidence was forthcoming. A tissue smeared with Munley's blood was found inside the pensioner's house. These samples were used to build-up a DNA profile of the as-yet unknown killer. Forensics expert Mr Peter Smith said that traces of Munley's DNA had been taken from tissues found at the scene of the crime. These were not only taken from the sample of blood but also saliva which was extracted from five cigarette butts found in the house. Mr Smith said there was only a one-in-five-billion chance that the DNA sample on the tissues and cigarettes would match the DNA profile of anyone else.

Munley denied ever having been in Miss Barnes's house and suggested that the police had framed him, planting his DNA sample in the house or switching samples during their transportation either from or to the forensics lab. The judge explained this to the jury: 'The suggestion is that some time between 9 March 1999 and 31 March 1999, a corrupt police officer, armed with a suitably tainted tissue, somehow gained access to the laboratory and seized the tainted tissue, switching it so that, on analysis, it would identify the defendant.'

At the end of the hearing, the jury were out for an extended period of discussion as they could not agree unanimously on the verdict. DS Steve Scott waited and sweated. The case had lasted for one-and-a-half years and cost around half-a-million pounds. His devotion to solving the case had cost a great deal in terms of manpower and budget and, although he was grateful to his whole team, not to mention Julian Boon and Audrey Ridpath, he was still unsure as to whether Munley would be found guilty. Eventually, the jury returned and delivered their verdict. They found him guilty.

The judge said that, as Munley continued to deny involvement in the murder, the truth about the pensioner's final hours will probably never be known. When the jury announced its unanimous guilty verdict, Munley went white and put his hands to his head. He was found guilty on one count of murder, seven counts of burglary and five counts of forgery. He was found not guilty on one count of burglary of a pair of candlesticks, which were never recovered.

Before sentencing him, Mr Justice Alliott told Munley that it was 'beyond belief' that he continued to burgle Miss Barnes as her body lay decomposing in the house. 'I am prepared to accept that this was not in any way a premeditated murder. It was committed by you in some confrontation with the elderly lady. The callousness in letting her lie as she fell and your degradation was beyond belief. You have shown no acceptance of guilt and not a flicker of remorse.'

Even though Munley denied ever having visited Miss Barnes's house, he was later found to have done decorating and other odd jobs for her in the past. When police searched Munley's flat, they found several documents belonging to Miss Barnes under the floorboards, including her Civil Service membership card.

A handwriting expert, Mr Kim Hughes, said he was convinced that cheques written to pay for milk and bread had been written by Munley. Munley had also opened Miss Barnes's bills and paid them for her. And the note allegedly written to the milkman was definitely by him. Mr Jeremy Gompertz, Counsel for the Prosecution, explained that handwriting analysis revealed how Munley had written it. He said, 'The note and the cheques were part of the defendant's attempts to deflect attention away from Tennyson Road and prevent the discovery of Miss Barnes's body, until either he had thought of it, or possibly until a time when the body had decayed so much that police would be unable to identify how she died.

After Munley had been sentenced to life imprisonment, Mr Jeremy Winn said, 'I feel nothing but contempt for this evil man. He is a swine. My aunt was a brilliant woman who led a very interesting life. I hope he spends his time in jail realising what he has done in ending the life of a very fine woman in this way.'

Two weeks after Munley's conviction, the two milkmen had still not received a letter telling them they were in the clear, let alone receiving an apology. And even though the killer was apprehended, the shadow of suspicion that they were still somehow involved in the murder had not been officially lifted.

After the trial, DS Steve Scott, who led the inquiry, said, 'Mrs Ridpath provided us with the vital clue we had been waiting for. I think she is an amazing woman. To be able to recognise that handwriting so long after she saw it for the first time is incredible.'

Mrs Ridpath, the widow of an RAF squadron leader, said, 'I am pleased that Munley got what he deserved. I am pleased to have helped. All I did was take a cheque book to the police. The reward is jolly nice. It is far more than I expected. I will give most of it to charity to help children in the African state of Rwanda. My son Norman has worked there and has seen the poverty. I think this money shows what happens when a member of the public helps the police following an appeal for information.

'I was just watching the news when I saw the preview for *Crimewatch*. Immediately, I recognised the handwriting as that of Munley as he had forged signatures to steal money from my neighbour's bank account. Luckily, we managed to get it back. I am glad I was able to help the police. My friends have been calling me Miss Marple ever since and I'm a bit fed up with it. I think it is a very good thing that the man was caught because, obviously, he would have done it again.'

10

THE SATURDAY NIGHT STRANGLER

The Top Rank nightclub in Swansea is packed to the limit with young revellers. The date is September 1973 and the dance floor is awash with knee-high platform boots, feather hairstyles and miniskirts. The speakers are thumping out the latest tunes from Marc Bolan as the mixture of young men and women dance wildly in the crush of bodies.

Upstairs, in the cinema, others are watching Roger Moore playing James Bond in *Live and Let Die*. An apt title as, in a few hours time, two of the people enjoying the merriment provided by the Top Rank Club that evening would be dead.

Great Britain at that time was in the throes of an energy crisis and soon the neon lights advertising the latest entertainment would be turned out by order of the Government. Soaring oil prices in the Middle East had put up energy prices and, at home, a miners' strike was causing coal reserves to run dangerously low. The Prime Minister, Edward Heath, ordered industry on to a three-day week to save power and to stave off power cuts.

PCs, CDs and microwaves had yet to be invented; the terms 'serial killer' and 'psychological profiling' had not yet been coined.

Yet somewhere in the Top Rank Club that evening a serial killer was on the prowl. Maybe he had already chosen his victims, or perhaps he sought a chance encounter. Whichever way the events unfolded, the evening would end with the violent rape and death of two young girls.

Geraldine Hughes and Pauline Floyd were having a great evening. They had spent considerable time on the dance floor, where their youthful enthusiasm could be exploited to the full. Geraldine was a fun-loving girl with lots of energy and had dressed for the night's entertainment in her favourite white mini-dress. Pauline, on the other hand, was quieter and smaller at just 5ft. She was sporting her new green nail varnish and an array of finger rings that were popular at the time. They were having a great evening and were disappointed when the internal club lights were switched on, signalling that it was time to go home.

Pauline and Geraldine lived some seven miles away from Swansea, their homes being in the neighbouring villages of Llandarcy and Skewen. It was always difficult returning home after a night out. They both worked in the local sewing factory and earned around £16 per week each, making the average £4 taxi fair home too great a price to pay. They would, unfortunately, have to pay a far greater price in due course.

At 1.00am, the girls emerged into the dark evening which had turned to a slow rain. They decide to take shelter at a local bus-stop just a few hundred yards from the club.

Philip O'Connor was driving along the road. He was also returning home although he wasn't in the habit of either offering people a lift or, indeed, picking up hitch-hikers. As he approached the bus-stop under which Geraldine and Pauline were sheltering, he was forced to brake as a creamy-white car in front of him swerved dangerously across the road to pull up in front of the two girls.

As O'Connor paused at the traffic lights, the other car pulled up alongside and he could see the two girls chatting away with the driver, who sported a bushy haircut and a large dark moustache, though the rest of his face was hidden by his passengers. When the lights changed, both cars pulled away and O'Connor thought no more of it. But he would over the coming years; he would think quite a lot about that moment, when both Geraldine and Pauline were unquestionably alive and action to prevent their deaths could have been taken. But no one, not even the girls themselves, realised there was any danger at the time.

The exact sequence of what happened next is hard to piece together. The driver of the car took the girls to a wooded copse near Llandarcy where both victims were beaten, raped and subsequently strangled. The next day, Pauline was discovered lying face down with her black platform boots beside her, a 5ft-long rope lashed several times around her neck and her clothes heavily bloodstained.

Fifty yards away lay the body of Geraldine, close to the main Jersey Marine Road, a route buzzing with traffic day and night. She also had a rope around her neck and both victims had suffered serious head wounds.

Both girls were fully clothed, although their feet were muddy inside their tights. Presumably, they had been allowed to dress following the rapes. The reason for this can only be guessed. Maybe the killer had not yet decided on murder; perhaps the girls were able to persuade him that they would not tell anyone and hence were allowed to dress; maybe the killer then had second thoughts and decided the only way to be sure of his anonymity was to silence them for ever. We will never know for sure, neither will we know how the killer managed to control his two victims while driving to the scene of the murder and while they were there.

At 10.00am the following day, pensioner Walter Watkins stumbled across Pauline's body while out walking. When the police arrived, they discovered Geraldine's a little further into the copse and so began one of the biggest police manhunts the area had ever seen. The murder squad consisted of 150 detectives, the most extensive force ever assembled in Welsh history.

Photos of the victims are shocking. Both girls look absurdly out of place, like mannequins, dumped from the back of a truck. On close up, their faces are covered with mud and look strangely aged by the agony of their violent deaths. It was indeed a horrific crime, and had been carried out in the heart of a particularly close-knit community.

Llandarcy is located in a densley populated area of South Wales, dominated by steel plants, oil refineries and deepwater docks. The men of the area are a hard breed, being used to the rigours of hard manual labour and yet, at the same time, are famous for close-knit families and communities. The towns of Swansea, Port Talbot and Neath are a short distance along the M4 corridor. This is a busy area, with a lot of passing traffic and large number of migrant workers and visitors.

The police began their enquiries and information was sought from the public. The road on that evening, as usual, was quite busy and it soon emerged that a car was seen protruding from the entrance to the copse somewhere between 1.45am and 2.15am on that Sunday morning. The car was identified as a white Austin 1100, although no one could recollect the licence number.

The murder squad was led by Chief Superintendent Ray Allen, who set up an incident room in Skewen Police Station. These were the days long before computers could be used to store and disseminate information, so the police had no choice but to rely on the manual, paper-based cardex system and a 'graticule' – a wall-sized white board divided into tiny squares in which individual enquiries or actions were listed and then crossed off when completed.

Early in the inquiry, a potential link to another murder was identified. Just three months earlier, a 16-year-old hitch-hiker, Sandra Newton, had been found strangled, her body dumped close to a local disused colliery. She, too, had been raped and had then been choked to death with the hem of her chiffon skirt. Sandra had been seen walking home from a night out in Briton Ferry, a neighbouring village, and once again there had been reports of a white Austin 1100 in the vicinity.

The murder squad were divided over this latest investigation. Could it possibly be linked to the double murder? The only connection at the time had been the sighting of the mysterious Austin 1100, being driven erratically around the time of the murder. It could, after all, be a coincidence. The number of cars matching that description was huge as that particular model was very much in vogue at the time.

Police discovered from friends that the victim had been involved with a married man at the time. When questioned, her lover admitted that they had gone to the nightclub on the evening of Sandra's murder and they had had sex in the back of an abandoned van. Following that, the man had rather ungallantly left Sandra at the roadside to make her own way home and, no doubt, she had also hitched a lift. Although suspicion was directed at Sandra's lover, police could find no motive.

It wasn't long before the newspapers had dubbed the elusive killer 'The Saturday Night Strangler', and the whole area was besieged by fear, partly as a result of a poster campaign run by the police, which read, 'DANGER, THUMBING LIFTS HAS LED TO MURDER – DON'T'.

The area was dominated by the presence of the police. Panda cars, police dog teams and officers on foot routinely patrolled the streets, increasing public anxiety, while at the same time providing a sense of protection.

A close friend of Pauline and Geraldine's said at the time, 'My mother would not let me out of her sight. The killer could have been the milkman, the postman, anyone.'

The intensive police investigation led to numerous reports being filed. The steelworks in Port Talbot alone employed more than 13,000 men. The M4 motorway was in the final phase of completion and this had drafted in hundreds of transient employees to meet the demand.

The Neath Fair had also been in the vicinity at the time of the murders, attracting many more visitors to the area.

The strongest lead of the case so far had been the white Austin 1100. At the time of the crimes, the local taxation office, where, at that time, cars had to be registered, showed there were about 11,000 cars matching the description. Each owner had to be visited and a statement taken, along with alibis and supporting evidence.

Soon the inquiry was drowning in its own paperwork and the details taken had to be painstakingly extracted manually. At Skewen, there were 35,000 index cards, containing names and different subject categories – 'queer person', 'rumours', 'psychopath', 'psychics', 'pregnant woman' and 'suspicious acts'. There were 10,500 nominal suspects, 11,000 car questionnaires, 4,000 statements from Austin car owners and a further 10,000 miscellaneous statements. The amount of information was overwhelming, making the job of cross-indexing and checking a supremely difficult and time-consuming task.

The police were certain that the killer was being shielded by family or friends. Given the evidence at the horrific murder scene, the killer must have returned home that night covered in blood, and no one other than a complete lunatic could have acted normally thereafter. The police organised a press conference, appealing for anyone with information to come forward. The police asked, 'Did you know someone who drove that type of car? Were they out on the evening of the murder? Were their shoes muddy? Did they behave differently, washing their own clothes, the car ... anything? The man we are hunting is sick and needs help. He could kill again unless he is caught without delay.'

The police investigation continued, sifting through all of the information that had been put together. A suspect at this time was called Joseph Kappen, a doorman who had worked at the Top Rank Club on the evening of the double murder and who also drove a white Austin 1100. The police spent considerable time interviewing Kappen. He was a known petty felon with a criminal record and he soon emerged as the prime suspect. Tall, muscular, with rugged good looks, spoiled only by his discoloured and rotten teeth, Kappen sported a drooping Mexican-style moustache. He was also a judo enthusiast, and was a well-known figure around the pubs and clubs of Port Talbot and Swansea. With his imposing size, Kappen was known to be a rough customer and was not afraid to mix it with trouble-makers. He also took advantage of his job to chat up single women and was known to be a predatory womaniser. One said, 'If it wasn't for his rotten teeth, he would have been quite good-looking.'

However, the police could never find enough evidence to make a formal charge. This situation was compounded by Kappen's wife, Christine, providing a suitable alibi for him, as and when needed.

Kappen had a record of minor offences, around 30 in total, for robbing gas meters, car thefts, burglary and assault. He had spent years in and out of prison. When not incarcerated, he would work as a driver on lorries or buses and, to supplement his income, he'd take casual work as a doorman in the evenings in the local pubs and clubs. He'd never been known to hold down a job for very long, preferring instead to receive social security, while earning cash on the side. He was also known to smoke cannabis and occasionally did a bit of dealing, but his real drug of choice was tobacco, which he both chewed and smoked, rolling some 20 Old Holborn roll-ups a day, enough to stain his teeth and ensure that his clothing reeked of stale smoke.

He was an archetypal loner. Lots of people knew of him, but no one, it would appear, *really* knew him. He would go out to pubs and clubs up to three times a week and was on a local darts team, but he didn't really drink, always preferring to stay in control.

Kappen was married to Christine, whom he had met when she was just 17 on the beachfront at Port Talbot. Christine says, 'It was 1962 and nobody had any money in those days. You'd go to a café, get a coffee for sixpence and hang out. It was September and cold. The first thing that attracted me to him was that he bought me a hot chocolate to warm my hands. It was the first kind thing anyone had ever done for me.'

Christine Powell was married to Kappen for 18 years before divorcing him in 1980. When they had first got together, Kappen was considered something of a catch. He was 6ft 1in, and had dark, Italian looks with slate-blue eyes. Long before it was ever fashionable, Kappen worked out with dumbbells and had developed an imposing physique. And, to top it all, he had a motor car, an obsession he would maintain over the years by becoming involved in car theft.

In the summer of 1963, Christine became pregnant with their daughter Deborah, and they got married the following February, but there was no time for a honeymoon – ten days after the wedding, Kappen was sent to prison for breaking into houses with the intention of robbing gas meters. For this, he was sentenced to three years. Deborah was born in April and in August Kappen was released on day parole to attend his stepfather's funeral. At the wake, while the warders were downstairs, Kappen cornered Christine in one of the bedrooms where they had sex. The result was Christine's second pregnancy with son Paul. By the time Kappen was finally released, he was the father of two children whom he had never met.

On his release, the Kappens moved to the Sandfields Estate, but it was not to be a happy household. Kappen never bonded with his children. They lived on social security and Christine found that she could not rely on her husband for money. They literally did not have two pennies to rub together, a situation not improved by Kappen's continual brushes with the law.

He had also started to hit Christine, who, lacking any other reference, had come to think the beatings were a normal way for a man to treat a woman. 'I thought all men were violent,' she later told police. 'He used to rape me every two weeks. I never wanted it, but Joe would insist upon his conjugal rights.' Rows were frequent in the Kappen household, and the police were regularly called to keep the peace, although at this time the police did not routinely get involved in what was considered to be a private domestic situation.

Later, a psychological profiler would highlight several characteristics common in a serial killer, all of which seemed chillingly accurate in respect of Joe Kappen. As the profile predicted, Kappen's hobbies were solo interests – rearing canaries, tropical fish and greyhounds. One of the greyhounds became a family pet. In a brief insight into the occasionally violent world of Kappen, he strangled one dog in front of his son Paul while out walking with the pet on a local beach, because he deemed the dog to be too old. He had a chilling temper and, on one occasion, sent out his children, Deborah and Paul, late, one wet evening, to find replacements for biscuits they had eaten at the house. As he would do with his future victims, Kappen ruled his family by terror.

Following a tip-off, detectives visited Kappen on 13 October 1973 at his house, nearly one month after the murders had occurred. Once again, Kappen passed through the system, claiming to have returned from Neath Fair at around 9.30pm on the Saturday, looking after his canaries until he and his wife went to bed at 10.45pm. Christine, sitting beside him on the sofa, simply agreed with his version of events. This was a usual occurrence, as far as she was concerned; the police were always round for one reason or another, and she had always provided the relevant protection, as wives often do. Besides, Kappen may have been a petty crook and an occasional wife-beater, but he could surely not have committed those crimes against the young girls in the papers.

Christine would later say, 'You learned to provide the alibis without thinking, saying, "On such and such a night, he was with me, officer."' And, as far as Christine knew, Joe Kappen had never displayed any unhealthy interest in young girls.

The truth was that Kappen regularly pursued young teenage girls. His job as a bouncer brought him into regular contact with the younger generation. People who knew him said, 'It was a thrill for him to go with younger girls, even when he was 43. If he had a girl, he would parade her around to impress his mates.' And, as far as is known, in bed it was always regular sex, nothing out of the ordinary.

As a bus driver on the local buses, Kappen would use his rest breaks on the local green to try and chat up the girls. He was a sexual predator, who always carried a knife and was known to have had a ligature with him at Llandarcy. He was always cocky, confident and unafraid of carrying out crimes in his own back yard.

Kappen's record of assaults on women, all unknown to the police at the time of the investigation, began in the early 1960s. In 1964, he attacked a 15-year-old schoolgirl as they were walking together in the Sandfields Estate. As they entered a half-built house, Kappen suddenly threw the girl to the ground and pounced on her. Luckily, the girl was able to scream out loud and Kappen decided to run off.

There were other incidents that look to have Kappen's particular stamp about them. In February 1973, a man resembling Kappen, in an Austin, picked up two female hitch-hikers near Neath. As they neared the drop-off point, he drove past and took them to an isolated road. One girl was seated in the front and the other was in the back. The attacker stopped the car and told them, 'I know you want it,' and he grabbed the girl in the front and started pawing her breasts. The girl in the back leaned forward to intervene but was hit squarely in the face with great force, knocking her violently back into the rear seat. Both girls were now screaming and trying to escape, but all the doors were inoperable from the inside. Fortunately, the girl in the back had long nails and was able to pull up the stub of the door lock and open the door. Jumping out, she opened the front door and the two continued screaming. The attacker noticed lights going on in a nearby house and, once again, fled the scene. The girls never reported the attacks for fear of recriminations.

The two girls were lucky; who knows what the outcome would have been if they had not been able to escape the car. Their attacker was almost certainly Kappen, but his next victim, Sandra Newton, would not fare so well.

By mid-1974, the inquiry had run out of leads, and with the available data not providing the opportunity of an arrest, the investigation was quietly wound down. To everyone's disappointment, it appeared that the Saturday Night Strangler had got away with it.

On the third anniversary of the murders, Geraldine Hughes's mother, Jean, led a protest march of 50 of her sewing factory workmates to number 10 Downing Street. There, they chanted for all to hear, 'Bring back hanging ...' The papers turned up and Mrs Hughes posed for photographers showing off the 9,000-signature petition, all in favour of bringing back the death penalty for those who had committed the ultimate crime. Mrs Hughes stormed, 'If they ever catch the person responsible, they should hang him. I want him to feel the rope around his neck like the girls felt.'

Sadly, even if the death sentence could be returned, there was no one in prison to go to the gallows. Back in South Wales, the trail had gone cold.

As we have seen in other cases, unsolved murders are never officially closed, so when the Llandarcy murder room was wound down, all of the evidence and information was sent to Sandfields Police Station in Port Talbot, where it lay undisturbed for the next 30 years, becoming damp, some of it turning into a black fungal mush. The most important evidence – the girls' underwear – would have the most forensic value, and was retained in the dry store rooms at the Home Office's forensic science labs in Chepstow, Gwent.

Over the ensuing years, the case was occasionally reviewed and the odd suspect brought in for questioning, but this was more a formality than any real investigative probing. Even the advent of DNA profiling in the mid-1980s had little impact, as the new technique required a fresh sample of DNA the size of a ten pence piece to provide any useful, dependable data. Stains on a victim's clothing from a decade earlier were of no use.

In the absence of progress, the victims' families remained in limbo. Mrs Hughes said of her daughter, 'Geraldine was full of life and gave us so much pleasure. She was the light of our lives and we have suffered the anguish of asking ourselves whether we should have allowed her out that night. The area has been tainted with these murders for years.'

The families struggled on through the years that followed, never really being able to move on from that night in 1973, perpetually haunted by the dreadful images of what happened, each desperate to know who had committed those vile crimes and longing for the delivery from their torment that might be found in a conviction.

Then, in 1998, the high-tech DNA LCN test was developed that could provide results from just a tiny speck of DNA material. The girl's clothing and swabs were sent to a specialist research lab in Birmingham for testing. This was a protracted process, as the killer's DNA was present somewhere in the 25-year-old samples. After two years of intensive work, the scientists could only obtain a partial profile of the killer's DNA, extracted from Geraldine. But the result from Pauline was unambiguous – a full genetic profile that could be expressed as a unique series of numbers was obtained. Now the police held the killer's genetic fingerprint, but had yet to put a face and a name to this person who had evaded capture for almost 30 years.

The criminal national DNA database (NDNAD) holds 1.7 million profiles, but the Llandarcy killer wasn't one of them. If the police wanted to catch the killer, they were going to have to go looking for him.

On 27 January 2000, some 27 years after the murders, the investigation into the Llandarcy murders was reopened, under the codename Operation Magnum. Although still a murder inquiry, it felt like the piecing together of some historical mystery. No crime ever had been solved so long after the actual event but, then again, no previous investigation had had the benefit of DNA LCN profiling.

The entire Magnum team consisted of just three people – Chief Inspector Paul Bethell and two ageing detectives, Phil Rees and Geraint Bale, both of whom had a 30-year service with the police. Bethell recreated the Llandarcy murder room in a run-down police station in Pontardawe, close to the murder scenes, from which they set out to catch the killer.

The grand plan was to DNA swab the most likely suspects and then to match them with the Llandarcy killer's profile. Bethell's problem was that he had been given sufficient budget to carry out just 500 of the expensive and time-consuming tests. Therefore, he had only one option – he and his detectives would need to go back through all the old paperwork and come up with the most likely suspects out of the 35,000 names that existed in the paper files.

Although a daunting task, the officers began sifting through the files and soon discovered a host of unsolved rapes in the Neath area. There was no DNA evidence as the women's clothing had been destroyed. However, two of the rapes, carried out in the months prior to the murders, had a strong similarity to the Llandarcy killings, because they involved the use of ropes.

The rapist lay in wait for his victims and then attacked them from behind, grabbing and hitting them, and threatening them until they submitted. He then tied them up and raped them. He was a cool, confident individual, smelled strongly of tobacco, had a moustache and wore a balaclava. After the attack, he would tell the victim to keep her eyes closed while he had a cigarette and decided if he was going to kill her.

The detectives also drew on another tool that was not available to the 1973 investigation team – the psychological profiler. The new Magnum team called in Rupert Heritage, former chief of the behavioural science unit of Surrey Police, to draw up a 14-point profile. The profile predicted that the Llandarcy killer would be white, aged late twenties to mid-thirties at the time of the attacks, have a record for minor property crime and would have come to the attention of the police as a juvenile. It was also likely that the killer would have a history of assaults and possible animal cruelty, and was, in all likelihood, from the Neath area. The man was unskilled and had an incomplete family background, such as an absent father, may have had an unhappy marriage, would collect weapons and have solo sports interests.

Using the profile as a reference point and a template to begin their daunting search, the Magnum team started whittling their way through the list of 35,000 names. For the next eight months, the detectives spent their time in the filing room, knowing that any mis-filing could ruin the chances of catching the killer. For a long time, no one on the team really thought they stood a chance of catching the killer; perhaps the killer's name wasn't even in that room with them, or maybe the killer had been an opportunist visitor, a foreigner who had come through the Swansea docks. The chances looked slim, but eventually the detectives came up with their 500 names.

Now came the task of locating the men on the list. Another logistical nightmare, as people move, get married, die and life generally moves on – but not for the families of those victims, still locked in 1973, hoping for a breakthrough.

The detectives used every conceivable official organisation to assist them in their task – they contacted the DVLA, the tax office and criminal records to locate people at addresses all over the globe, even as far away as New Zealand. After locating the potential suspect, they had to persuade each one to volunteer his DNA. As Chief Inspector Bethell says, 'We were looking for a particular tree in a forest. In order to find it, you had to cut down all of the other trees. The beauty of DNA is that you can once and for all eliminate a suspect.'

Over the next eight months, the detectives were able to persuade 353 men to give DNA swab samples. Of course, a refusal would have immediately triggered further police suspicion, and most suspects were not at all pleased to be asked questions regarding a 30-year-old sex murder case.

As the DNA test results started to come back, they all indicated negative matches. The detectives were now forced to review their approach. The 500 nominal suspects had been prioritised into five groups. The first 50 swabs were of witnesses, relatives, stepfathers, boyfriends, anyone who had featured prominently in the original investigation. After these came ordinary criminal suspects.

Each swabbing operation, even if it failed, generated its own trail of paperwork. Typical of this was nominal suspect number 200, one Joe Kappen, who lived on the Sandfields Estate in Port Talbot. In August 2001, Detective Rees went to the address and knocked on the door. Kappen's now ex-wife Christine answered the door. Christine Powell was still living at the address, but Joe Kappen was not. He had been dead 11 years. Kappen had been diagnosed with lung cancer during 1988 and had died in 1990, spending the last few months of his life in a wheelchair, a frail ghost of the man he used to be. He had subsequently been buried in the family grave.

Rees, on cross-checking with the local death register, reallocated Kappen to the dead pool, those awaiting final elimination from the inquiry by cross-checking with family members' DNA – another long and tedious task.

Two months later, the Magnum team had a breakthrough. A DNA specialist, Dr Jonathan Whitacker, managed to extract a profile from swabs taken from Sandra Newton's body. It was a three-way mix. The profile showed the DNA material was from Sandra, her boyfriend and an unknown individual. The DNA from the unknown person on the Sandra Newton murder matched DNA material of the killer in the Llandarcy case. It was the same killer; finally, they were able to confim with absolute certainty that the killer of Geraldine and Pauline was also responsible for the murder of Sandra. Sandra's body had been dumped in a water culvert so remote and well hidden that its whereabouts would only have been known to locals.

With this new knowledge, Rees finally felt that they would locate the killer. He lived in the local area, and therefore had to be on the list and he had driven an Austin 1100.

In October 2001, Whitaker came up with another original thought. 'We get 50 per cent of our genetic material from each parent. The offender could have had children ... maybe there was a relative of the offender on the database. On the basis that we get half of our DNA material from each parent, we therefore had 50 per cent of the killer's children's DNA profile as well.'

Whitaker spent another long period searching the stored profiles on the NDNAD system, eliminating thousands of names in the process. This was a unique line of investigation; the detectives were attempting to identify the killer's DNA through his children.

One of the shortlist of 100 immediately sprang to the fore, one Paul Kappen, a petty car thief, who would have been only seven years old at the time of the Llandarcy killings. But two Kappens in the files was just too much of a coincidence – Joe Kappen, having died 12 years earlier, was the number-one suspect.

Pursuing this line of investigation vigorously, Rees and Bale returned to the Sandfields Estate and persuaded Christine and her daughter Deborah to provide DNA swabs. By subtracting Christine Powell's DNA from her son's and daughter's, the forensic scientists would be able to recreate most of Joe Kappen's DNA profile.

The process took a further two weeks for the results to come through. Bethell, who was sat at his desk in the Pontardawe murder room, remembers the moment. 'The call came through from the forensic scientist, Colin Dark. He was going on about a partial match and the DNA banding. And I said, "What are you telling me?" And he replied, "I think you have got your man." It was a strange feeling, very emotional. I don't get excited or overwhelmed, not after all these years. But I really did get a lump in my throat.'

What the scientist had got was a three-quarters profile of Kappen that was identical to that of the Llandarcy killer. Statistically, it was him, but murder inquiries are not a game of statistics. The team really wanted to be able to tell the families of the victims that the man in the grave was definitely the man responsible for their daughters' deaths.

On Christmas Eve 2001, Bethell made an application to the Home Secretary, David Blunkett, to exhume the body of Joe Kappen. In death, Kappen was making history as the first serial killer ever to be pulled from his grave to ascertain his guilt.

The permission to dig up Joe Kappen from his communal grave in Goytre Cemetery took a further five months to come through. When it did, the final chapter in the case of the Llandarcy killings and another could be written.

The families were told of the breakthrough. Retired oil refinery engineer Mr Hughes said at his Llandarcy home, 'When we heard about the police breakthrough, we couldn't believe it at first. We were so shocked, my wife and I broke down and cried all night. We took flowers to

Geraldine's grave and had a few quiet words with her and felt we had put her to rest properly.'

Geraldine's parents had always clung to the hope that one day the killer would be found. Mrs Hughes said, 'The news of the police breakthrough gave us an overwhelming sense of relief. Our tears were the pent-up outpouring of emotions after so long.'

It was a retired Port Talbot detective, Elwyn Wheadon, who had given Kappen's name to the original murder team. Wheadon has said, 'Kappen was a bouncer in nightclubs. He was a man with a violent disposition, a Fagin-like character who sought out boys and girls to commit crimes on his behalf. I first met him at a youth club where he had thrown a boy down some stairs. There were no injuries, but you knew Kappen was capable of anything, and I knew he had an Austin 1100.'

The moment of conclusion was fast approaching. By 15 May 2002, the exhumation team, forensic archaeologists, forensic dentists, pathologists and policemen were finally ready. A large blue tent was erected around the grave and, as dusk fell, the digging started, under the blue-white glare of police arc lights. The first coffin to be raised was that of Kappen's stepfather. Thus far, 15 May had been a fine day but, as the team finally found the coffin of Kappen, the clouds rolled in and thunder and lightning raged across the sky like some old-style horror movie. Kappen had died of lung cancer aged 49 and, after leaving Christine, he had become involved with a local barmaid, Sandra Wyatt. They set up home on the Baglan housing estate and, according to Wyatt, he had hardly left the house during his latter years.

Kappen's coffin was finally dragged to the surface intact.

It was removed to a local mortuary and opened. The team finally came face to face with their suspect, some 30 years after the crime. Teeth and one femur were removed, the areas most likely for DNA material to survive. The findings were then sent for analysis, and the body was put back into the grave, following a small service.

Three weeks later the test results came back, and proved once and for all that the killer had been Kappen. The Magnum team had mixed feelings; there was a feeling of anti-climax: the killer was dead, so there would be no trial and no retribution.

The information was passed to other forces who had also had unsolved rapes and murders, as it seemed unlikely that Kappen had committed only the offences that had come to light so far. Humberside Police reported that they were re-examining the disappearance of nine-year-old Christine Markham, from Robinson Road, Scunthorpe. She had vanished on 21 May 1973 and had not been seen since. It was known that, during the period of August to September 1973, Kappen had lived in the Gainsborough area, while working as a contract driver.

A number of investigations continue at the time of writing.

11

GUILT ON A SLIDE

[illegible]

Anne Crofts and her daughter Sarah were worried. Pacing up and down the front room of their house at Basingbourne Close, Fleet, in the picturesque county of Hampshire, they were desperate for the appearance of Anne's younger daughter, Marion, after she had cycled the five miles to Wavell School, North Camp, Farnborough. It was Saturday, 6 June 1981, a bright day and good for a bike ride. Marion had set off with her clarinet at around 9.00am and was due to be home by 3.30pm ... it was now well after 4.00pm. Marion was a serious girl who did well at school and who was normally a reliable timekeeper. Her out-of-character lateness was creating something of a panic in the Crofts household.

Unable to contain themselves any longer, Anne and her daughter decided to cycle in the direction that Marion would be travelling when returning home. Leaving their home, they cycled a while and eventually turned into Laffans Road in Aldershot, which leads down to the the Basingstoke Canal, along which Marion would have travelled earlier that day, and where they were hopeful of bumping into her on her way home.

Those expectations were cruelly dashed when Anne noticed a sponsorship form on the ground. She couldn't be sure, but it looked like the one Marion had with her that morning when she had set off. A sudden nervousness set in, and a deep fear gave her a queasy feeling in her stomach.

A few moments later, the nervousness turned to terror as Anne came across a plimsoll and a sock. She stared at the items strewn on the ground. They were Marion's, no doubt about it, and now Anne and Sarah knew something terrible had happened.

With the speed that only a fear-induced adrenalin rush can provide, they raced across to the Army Golf Club and immediately telephoned the police, but, as Anne waited for them, she was already dreading the worst. The police arrived with a sniffer dog. That sight did nothing to allay the growing fears of Anne and Sarah Crofts who by now were frantic, tearful and losing hope. Those scattered belongings could surely have only one meaning. They waited for the police to conclude their search.

Sadly, they did not have long to wait. At 5.20pm, a police dog-handler found the battered body of Marion Crofts in a copse alongside Laffans Road, adjacent to the Basingstoke Canal and close to the Army Golf Club, from which Anne had called the police.

Anne Crofts was devastated, now condemed to a nightmare world of regret and self-reproach for the next

20 years. Marion's father was playing cricket on that Saturday evening when the police arrived and called him off the pitch. Recalling that fateful moment, he says, 'As soon as the officers came for me, I knew something had happened to Marion. When they asked me to go to the police station, I realised she was dead.'

Hampshire Police launched an investigation, led by DS John Carruthers. The search was now on for a killer who had inflicted severe injuries on an innocent child, then raped and finally beaten her to death. At the time, Carruthers said, 'This is one of the nastiest cases I've seen. On a scale of one to ten, it has to be a ten. Everyone associated with the case has been affected.'

The day after the discovery of Marion's body, a canoeist on the Basingstoke Canal found a clarinet case floating by the edge. This was shown to have belonged to Marion and, on further searching, the police pulled a blue Jetstream racing bike, with drop handles and multi-gears, from the bottom of the canal, not far from where the body had been found.

Tony Jasinskyj, an army chef based near Aldershot, sat on the floor playing with his baby daughter. His wife Lynn looked on with mixed feelings. There he was, playing with their child, and only a few days earlier he had given Lynn a severe beating. It was true to say she no longer loved Jasinskyj; indeed, she was quite pleased looking at him sitting there with scratches all over his arms. For once, someone had given him a taste of his own medicine, she thought – a real good hiding – and no one deserved it more than him. However, unbeknown to Lynn, those scratches had not been inflicted by another man, they were the result of dragging the body of Marion Crofts into the dense undergrowth after he had ruthlessly murdered her. But the truth would not be revealed to Lynn or their children for another 20 years, during which period she would divorce him on the grounds of physical cruelty, and eventually remarry.

The forensic team had been called in to collect as many samples as they could. The area was combed and Marion's clothing was stored safely in air-tight plastic bags. Scrapings had been transferred on to slides and these, too, were put aside for long-term safekeeping. In the early eighties, the science of DNA profiling was in its infancy and it would be many years before the secrets locked into that molecular structure could be revealed. However, the police and the scientists had faith that, at some point, that particular branch of science would make a breakthrough that might just crack the case.

Meanwhile, the police conducted a broad-ranging investigation. The army barracks were within a couple of miles and housed a lot of men, a serious consideration in a case which was primarily driven by rape. Over the weeks, more than 24,000 statements were taken from people living in and around the area, with 1,500 of them coming from soldiers stationed at the barracks. But even after such a sweeping inquiry, the police were unable to identify any likely suspects. Tony Jasinskyj had also been one of those who completed a statement, in which he claimed to have been at work on the day of the murder.

The facts that emerged shocked a public who were already used to reading of horrific attacks. Marion had been riding her bike on that fateful morning along Laffans Road, when she was stopped by her killer. The exact details of the crime shall never be known fully, but what is known is that she was pulled off her bike, probably from behind. The pathology examination found marks around her mouth consistent with a hand being placed tightly across the lips. Marion was then pulled towards the copse where she was brutally beaten with fists and feet, so ferociously that her head had been driven into the ground, leaving a depression some two-and-a-half inches deep. She was then sexually assaulted, with death being caused by strangulation. In a lame bid to hide the crime, the killer had pulled Marion's body into dense undergrowth and threw her bike and clarinet into the canal.

Stunned by the ferocity of an attack on a girl so young, the police broadened their investigation. A police spokesman at the time said, 'The murder of Marion Crofts leads anyone in the police service to the conclusion that it is highly probable that the killer is responsible for other serious crimes. We would consider him to be someone who represents a very serious threat to the public.'

Each and every statement taken by the police was checked for reliability but nothing emerged to give the police a solid lead. The crime was reconstructed and the public were given another chance to have their memories jogged. From this process, a number of possible lines of enquiry began to emerge. A man with a red setter dog had been seen walking towards Eelmoor Bridge on the canal towpath between 9.00am and 9.30am that Saturday morning. He was described as around 6ft in height, wearing an anorak with a hood and carrying a stick. The owner of a brown or maroon Mark 3 Cortina was sought, as the car had been parked on Laffans Road on a number of consecutive Saturdays. This could, of course, just as easily have belonged to a jogger. Another driver was seen several times on Laffans Road between 9.30am and 11.00am, driving a Reliant three-wheeled car. A man was seen running down Laffans Road towards Eelmoor Bridge between 9.30am and 10.30am. He was 5ft 8in tall approximately, with dark hair and casually dressed. At 10.00am on the same morning, a youth aged about 16, wearing a blue cycle jacket, was seen cycling along the canal towpath towards Fleet. A host of other sightings were reported by members of the public, but the police were unable to trace any of the individuals, as the people who had been seen failed to come forward to be eliminated from the inquiry. The killer had been lucky not to have been witnessed in the act with so much activity going on in the locality, yet no one was able to provide that one vital clue for the breakthrough.

As the months passed, the police encountered one dead end after another. The real clues, Marion's clothing and the forensic material that had been transferred to laboratory slides, would not be able to shed light on the attack for many years to come. And so, during 1983, the police quietly scaled down the investigation, having exhausted all the possible leads that were available. Every so often, something would crop up and the core team working on the Marion Crofts case would spring back to life but, in the end, they yielded very little in the way of a breakthrough. At this stage, the killer had got away with one of the most despicable crimes the Hampshire force had ever investigated. The case had affected the officers involved in the investigation and no one, other than Marion's parents, was more upset and annoyed at the lack of progress.

In a twist of unnatural justice, it was the family of

Marion Crofts who paid the price each and every waking hour as the years passed. Mr Crofts blamed himself. 'What in life could be worse? If only I had taken her that morning. If only I had not gone to play cricket. But I will have to live with that every day for the rest of my days.'

The couple, who have two other daughters and a son, tried to move on with their lives but, as Mrs Crofts said, 'You don't forget. I think the worst time is probably on her birthday and when we have a sort of family occasion and the family is just not complete any more. She was a good pupil at school. She was a serious child, very musical and wanted to be a teacher.'

Marion's murder dealt a heavy blow to such a close family, and it had a prolonged influence over their day-to-day lives for the years that followed. Each member of her family couldn't help imagining the perpetrator walking the streets, enjoying his freedom, probably never even of thinking of Marion again after he had attacked and murdered her. He may not even have known her name. But worse was the prospect of picking up the papers one day and reading of a similar attack by the same person. The police had always indicated that the attack on Marion was not likely to be the first or the last of the man's crimes. Across all the time that had elapsed, the one thing that was missing, the one thing that would allow them some release, some sense of getting back to normal, was knowing who had killed Marion and that he would be behind bars for the rest of his days. But this would not happen for some time.

As the trail went cold, there seemed little prospect of ever finding the murderer. There did not appear to be any further crimes that could be linked to Marion's death, and so the case became increasingly dormant. However, the police did review the case once in a while, double-checking to see if anything had emerged that could throw new light on the situation. The case was brought back out of mothballs in 1995, and then again in 1997. During 1998, forensic scientists had finally developed DNA LCN, described in detail in an earlier chapter, which enabled the FSS to establish an accurate DNA profile from tiny amounts of forensic material that had been left at the scene, on weapons or clothing or on the victim during an attack.

With the advent of the new profiling technique, the police reopened the Marion Crofts murder inquiry, hoping to obtain some new evidence to identify the killer. Scientists from the FSS were given authority from the police to revisit the slides that had been prepared in 1981, some 18 years earlier. As the scientists said at the time, 'The slides are like tiny time-capsules. No one had looked at them since the time they were placed in the DNA archives to the time they were retrieved to undergo DNA LCN procedures.'

The procedure was to be a 'one shot' opportunity. If the procedure failed, they would not be able to use the slides again. The specialist DNA team at Trident Court obtained the slides and began their careful examination of the contents. The long-awaited breakthrough came in July 1999 when the police were informed by FSS scientists that a full DNA profile had been obtained. The results confidently predicted that the profile was accurate to the ratio of one in a billion. This then meant that only six people on the entire planet could match the DNA profile. Elated with the breakthrough, the police reopened the inquiry, now led by DS Andy Longman, who approached Mr and Mrs Crofts with the good news.

However, the investigation was to run into dead ends. The profile was run against the 17,000 profiles held on the police DNA database. There had always been a strong feeling among members of the police force that the killer of Marion Crofts had probably commited other serious crimes, so there were high hopes that his profile would be among those already stored. After a long and nervous wait, the results came up negative. The killer was not someone known to them previously, at least not someone who had been brought in for offences that involved some degree of violence. This was, however, only one of the avenues left open to the new murder squad.

During August 2001, police officers launched Operation Vortex, and began revisiting those people originally questioned during 1981 and 1982, eliminating those who were in the area at the time and who couldn't have been the killer. But, equally, there was the task of ruling out those who now, certainly, could have been. Officers from the Hampshire force sought out those men with the intention of taking a mouth swab and subjecting it to DNA analysis. In total, some 850 swabs were taken from people who were now living as far away as America and Australia.

In addition to the task of taking swabs, the police also interviewed and eliminated thousands of suspects, taking a further 3,321 statements. Unfortunately, once again the trail began to go cold, as it was shown that none of the individuals who had given mouth swabs could be the killer.

In a bid to give some final impetus to the inquiry, the

police decided to approach the BBC's *Crimewatch* programme. They appealed for names of anyone who could be the killer, or who could be in any other way connected to the murder of Marion Crofts. DS Andy Longman said on the programme, 'We need to hear from people who did not come forward at the time of the original inquiry and from people who may wish to alter or add to statements they gave 19 years ago.'

During the programme, four questions were asked for the public to consider: Did you kill Marion Crofts? Do you know who killed Marion Crofts? Did you make an alibi statement for someone which you are unhappy about? Do you have doubts about anyone you did not tell us about in 1981?

In addition, police had also issued a psychological profile of the killer. The profile was drawn up by psychologist Dr Julian Boon and transmitted to give the public yet more information to consider. But, once again, the response was disappointing; no new information was received and no match could be found for the killer's profile. By 23 August 2001, the police were once again preparing to wind down the inquiry.

By 2001, 20 years had elapsed since Marion had been killed. To Tony Jasinskyj, it must have been a distant memory, and he must surely have thought that the chances of being caught were not much more than zero. It is not known whether he saw the *Crimewatch* programme, whether mention of Marion's name brought all the memories flooding back, and whether for some time afterwards he worried that perhaps each knock on the door was by an arresting officer.

What we do know is that, after the murder, Jasinskyj

got on with his life. Indeed, he had returned home and played with his children not long after the attack. He continued to be violent towards his wife Lynn, occasionally leaving her with cuts and bruises. He also became a lorry driver, an activity that somehow lends itself to those prone to opportunistic killings, although proof of this has never emerged.

In another violent outburst, Jasinskyj beat and raped Lynn. She visited her solicitor and reported the incident, but domestic violence confined to the home was an area of the law that at this time was lacking. After putting up with his tendency towards violence for eight years, she finally left him and filed for divorce during 1984. Jasinskyj later married for a second time – to Michelle Jordan – whereupon they moved to Leicester and he continued his trade as a lorry driver. Having learned nothing from the break-up of his first marriage, he gradually settled back into a life of domestic disharmony. Once again, he was violent towards his wife and it was this violent streak that would ultimately prove his downfall.

In a fit of rage one evening, he overstepped the mark and hit Michelle about the face causing cuts and bruises. Michelle responded to the situation in the only way she could. She phoned the police and made an official complaint, saying she had been physically assaulted. The police arrived at the address and could see for themselves that Michelle bore all the hallmarks of a violent attack. Jasinskyj was taken to the police station and cautioned, during which he was given a routine mouth swab. He was released and the swab was analysed and the results entered into the police DNA database.

No one expected anything from the entry of the DNA

results, so the police force in Leicester were taken aback when the results of the tests positively matched against an existing record ... and they were even more amazed when they realised the man they had just released was probably the murderer of Marion Crofts some two decades earlier. The Hampshire Police Force were notified of the findings and Jasinskyj was arrested at his home in Kegworth Avenue, Leicester, on 3 September 2001, and formally charged with the murder and rape of Marion Crofts.

Anne and Trevor Crofts were informed of the breakthrough. They were told of the significant weight of the forensic evidence against Jasinskyj and the police were finally able to come face to face with the man they had been hunting for over two decades.

Dr Jonathon Whitaker, who carried out the DNA tests for the FSS, said at the time, 'This is a shining example of how forensic technology and DNA intelligence, in partnership with dedicated policing, effectively progressed the investigation into one of the most complicated and serious undetected crimes spanning two decades'.

During the interviews that followed, Jasinskyj maintained his innocence, against a backdrop of undisputable evidence. Beyond the DNA match, the police were able to prove that he lived one-and-a-half miles away from the murder scene, while stationed at the army barracks in Aldershot. In addition, his arrest for beating up his second wife was a testament to his willingness to use violence. Everything seemed to stack up.

Shortly after his arrest, the police visited his first wife Lynn, who was, by this time, remarried and living in Farnborough. They were calling to inform her that the father of her two grown-up daughters wasn't just a wife-beater but also a killer. Lynn remembers the day clearly. 'When a detective came to see me and told me what he had done, I knew in my heart exactly when he had done it.

'I went cold inside – full of horror because I'd been pleased at the time that this man who never got into fights with other men had finally got the smacking I dreamed of giving him every time he hurt me. But then here I was, 20 years on, learning that the marks and spatters of blood had been because of the attack and rape of a child – a little girl who couldn't defend herself. I had been to my solicitors because of his violence, but nothing was done. I felt so guilty. Could I have stopped this terrible thing happening if I had just made them listen to me? That day he had come back home and played with our first child for ages with scratches all over his arm. It was as if nothing out of the ordinary had happened. I don't understand how he could, knowing what he had just done to someone else's daughter. There he was, sitting on the floor with our little girl, playing the perfect daddy, yet he had just raped and murdered another little girl.'

After receiving the news from the police, Lynn offered to give a full, damning statement and attend court to help hammer the last few nails into his coffin.

Detectives who interviewed Jasinskyj, then aged 46, described his demeanour as cold and chilling. Even before the case came to court, psychological profiler Julian Boon said, 'Whoever committed this crime does not have the capicity for remorse in the same sense that you or I would understand the term. It is possible that he has committed other offences as serious as this one. I don't see this one in any way as being a peak.'

Lynn says, 'Looking back on our marriage, it was always violent, except when he was trying to charm me at the start. He'd split my lip a few times but always managed to talk me round and promised he would never do it again. Like a fool, I believed him. Now I understand why most women who are beaten stay in their relationships. Where would they go? How would they manage for money? I'd miscarried an earlier baby and so, the minute I knew I was pregnant with our second daughter, I refused to have sex with him. I began to worry that Marion's death was maybe my fault. Maybe it was the ban on sex that sent him out looking for someone.'

Telling her children that their father was a murderer was one of the hardest things Lynn has ever had to do. The fact that their daughters didn't know their father was, in retrospect, something of a blessing. If he had taken them out on trips and nice childhood holidays, his arrest may have destroyed treasured memories, which they may have found unbearable.

At Winchester Crown Court, Jasinskyj pleaded not guilty to the rape and murder of Marion Crofts, and maintained an unemotional disposition, his face displaying nothing of what was going on inside his head. At the time of the murder, Jasinskyj, like 1,500 other soldiers, had been asked to fill out a questionnaire about Marion's death. On it, he denied ever having been near the place where she was killed and claimed he was at work at the time. But Jasinskyj was lying.

When questioned about how his bodily fluids had ended up at the crime scene, he said that they had been planted there, like many other criminals do when faced with irrefutable evidence.

The jury of seven men and five women heard 21 days of evidence and reached their verdict on the second day of deliberations. A verdict of guilty was returned and Judge Michael Broderick jailed Jasinskyj for life for the murder of Marion and ten years for her rape, the sentences to run concurrently. In summing up, Judge Broderick said, 'The anguish that your action must have caused her parents, her family and friends probably cannot be imagined.'

Roger Daw, Chief Prosecutor for Hampshire and the Isle of Wight, said, 'I am extremely pleased that the Crown Prosecution Service has secured a conviction in this case, which has resolved a long-running murder inquiry undertaken by Hampshire Police. It is only because of huge advances in scientific evidence, and particularly through the examination of the defendant's DNA, that we were able to launch this prosecution. The jury's verdict has clearly demonstrated the significance of such evidence, notwithstanding the defendant's total denials. The CPS team worked extremely hard to put the best possible prosecution case before the court in a fair and professional manner and all their efforts have been vindicated. I sincerely hope that the family of Marion Crofts can now begin to put their long wait for justice behind them.'

The Crofts family also released a statement. 'Today marks the end of 20 years of agony for our family. The agony of wondering who killed Marion and wondering if he is still out there. The pain of her death remains – no verdict will bring Marion back to us. Nevertheless, we are grateful that her killer has been brought to justice. We hope that our family can now get on with our lives without the worry that Marion's killer is still at large. At times, it was hard for us to see what good the investigation was so many years after Marion's death. But, having heard the evidence against her killer, we are relieved that he is no longer a free man.'

In contrast to all the evidence presented in court, the facts and indisputable proof of Jasinskyj's activities, it is noteworthy to consider how, after such a violent attack, with all of the ensuing TV coverage, a man could remain undetected, giving virtually nothing away through his demeanour. We have heard how, subsequent to the murder, Lynn Jasinskyj could detect nothing unusual in his behaviour. Friends at the time and since have also described Jasinskyj at the time. A 33-year-old colleague, who did not want to be named, said, 'Once, when I was having a few money problems, I put Tony up for a few days. He wasn't a problem, he was out working most of the time. Although Jasinskyj always seemed cheerful and happy, he missed his wife and children and used to talk about them all of the time. He just slept a lot, got up, smoked a lot, ate a bowl of Cheerios and played the guitar, then went to work.'

But the colleague said he would never forget the day when Jasinskyj was arrested over the murder. 'It was unbelievable. I feel like a bad judge of character. I just knew him as a nice guy.'

Another friend said that they never had any suspicions about the dark secrets in Tony's past, one describing him as 'the nicest guy you could ever meet – he would do anything to help anybody'.

The statements of friends and collegues clearly show the difficulty in establishing guilt in those who are able to hide it through either split personality or, worse, a completely cold and chilling detachment from the crimes they have committed.

While Jasinskyj remains in jail, several police forces continue to investigate a string of other related sex offences and violent acts for which he may have been responsible during the 20 years of freedom he enjoyed while remaining undetected.

12

FALSE CONFESSION

The slightly built young man with the thin moustache stepped forward and took a seat opposite the medic, then began to roll up his shirt sleeve. The medic took a cursory glance at the visitor's passport to check his identity. If there was anything amiss, it failed to register with him.

A quick dab on the man's arm with a swab of cotton wool followed by the piercing of his skin with a hypodermic syringe, and a buccal swab rubbed on the inside of his cheek – and the medic's duty was done.

The samples of blood and saliva now extracted, they were placed in a plastic container, labelled, and then slid into a polythene bag to be despatched to the forensics lab by the next delivery.

'Sign here, please,' said the medic and the young man did as requested.

He leaned forward and wrote his signature on the dotted line. It read 'Colin Pitchfork'.

It had been the first mass blood sampling of its kind in Britain. The brainchild of DI Derek Pearce, who had been appointed head of the reopened investigation into the murders of two local girls, it was aimed at testing all men aged between 17 and 34 without strong alibis, who were residents of the three close-knit Leicestershire villages of Narborough, Enderby and Littlethorpe.

There was growing pressure from the Chief Constable and the Home Office to wind up the expensive inquiry, one way or another.

It was a last-ditch attempt to find the person responsible. Now, due to advances in genetic fingerprinting, it had been scientifically proven that both rapes and murders had been committed by the same man. With this recent advance in forensic science, a DNA profile of the killer had been drawn up, and now all the police had to do was find the match to the profile, and therefore find their killer.

Many of the police knew that the killer might evade the testing by substituting a volunteer to give a sample in his place, particularly with the presentation of identification without photographs such as driving licences, but it was a chance they had to take. They had neither the time nor the manpower to double-check the identity of each subject through follow-up interviews with them.

The two murders – three years apart – had shocked villagers, who thought that the killer still lurked in their midst.

On Monday, 21 November 1983, 15-year-old Lynda Mann, who lived in the village of Narborough, told her mother that she was going to visit two schoolfriends and would be back home by 10.00pm.

It had been a cold, frosty night with a full moon as she set out on her visit. Arriving at the first friend's house, she paid her friend's mother £1.50 towards the cost of a donkey jacket (which she was wearing at the time) bought from a clothes catalogue. Then she left to visit a second friend's house to pick up a record. She left there at close to 7.30pm.

The route which Lynda took to her friend's house is a footpath known locally as the Black Pad, sandwiched between the grounds of the Carlton Hayes Psychiatric Hospital and a new housing estate.

Her mother, Kathleen, and stepfather, Edward Eastwood, had spent the evening at a local pub, and had returned to find no sign of Lynda. Edward made a quick tour of the streets, including part way along the Black Pad footpath, before returning home and calling the police. The police registered the Missing Persons call at 1.30am. Although the police made an immediate search of the area, they could find no trace of the missing girl.

At 7.20am the next morning, a hospital porter was on his way to work at the Carlton Hayes Psychiatric Hospital, and noticed a figure lying in the hospital grounds. He thought it may be a mannequin of some description but was not sure so he ran into the road and flagged down an ambulance driver. They both returned along the path and peered through the railings. When they realised it was a girl's body, they phoned the police.

When they found the body, police roped off the area and erected a canvas shield around the site. Lynda Mann was lying face up in the grass. Her clothing lay in a pile a few feet away – shoes, pants and jeans. She was still wearing her donkey jacket and her scarf that had been pulled tight around her neck.

A pathologist from the Home Office conducted a post-mortem the next day at Leicester Royal Infirmary. Rigor mortis had already set in. He discovered blood around the nostrils and abrasions to the chin and front of the neck, along with some bruising to the upper chest. There were soil marks on her heels indicating that she had been dragged along the ground at some point. Lynda had probably been knocked unconscious with a single punch. The killer had obviously kneeled on her chest to strangle her; her unbroken fingernails were proof that she had been unable to fight for her life.

From semen samples taken from the body, forensics could at least narrow the search down by establishing the killer's blood group, particularly as it was a fairly rare type. The blood group was known as 'A' Secretor, classified as PGM 1+, which considerably reduced the range of possible suspects to about one tenth of the male adult population of the country. And the high sperm count discovered in the semen samples indicated a young man aged between 13 and 34. DCS David Baker, head of Leicestershire CID, placed DI Derek Pearce in charge of the inquiry. Pearce knew that the murderer could either be a local person or perhaps even a transient visitor, driving off the M1 to murder somewhere at random. However, he did consider it highly significant that Lynda Mann's body was found in the hospital grounds. Could the killer be one of the 600 mentally disturbed inmates?

They set up an incident room in a house belonging to the hospital and proceeded to interview every one of the staff and patients. There were also several hundred part-time patients who could come and go as they pleased, and they would know the grounds better than most outsiders. Even if one of them wasn't the killer, they may have seen something on the night of the murder which could prove vital to the police. These inmates and day-care patients formed a high proportion of the initial suspects, for many had a history of sexual offences. All local offences, ranging from rapes to indecent exposures, were fed into the police computers to form a reference bank against which to check names that might surface during the enquiries.

A 150-strong squad of murder detectives and police officers interviewed residents of Narborough and its adjacent villages of Littlethorpe and Enderby.

When Lynda Mann's body was released for burial in February 1984, CID men videoed mourners at the funeral at All Saints Church, thinking perhaps that one of them may be the killer. However, they were gradually losing confidence that they would single out a local man for the rape and murder. Appeals had been run through newspapers and TV, and any leads were chased up, all of which turned out to be false trails, which wasted many hours of investigation time.

There were several witness statements. There were persistent reports that a youth with a spiky, punk-style haircut had been seen with a girl dressed like Lynda near the scene of the murder on the night in question, but this was never substantiated and remained a perplexing mystery throughout. The police appealed for other people who had been seen in the vicinity of the Black Pad footpath to come forward so they could be eliminated from the enquiries, including a mystery jogger and a couple in a bus shelter. A video of the investigation was even made by detectives and shown in schools, discos and on shopping precincts, but no new leads were forthcoming. In August 1984 – less than a year after the murder – police had to admit that the trail had gone cold, and the investigation was officially called off.

Two-and-a-half years later, however, the murder of Lynda Mann had not faded away from the memories of local residents. Inhabitants of the three villages, particularly the parents, were very wary about where their children were, warning their teenage daughters to keep away from lonely paths and not to stay out too late. There was the possibility that the killer was from another area of Britain and that this had been a random attack, but the feeling prevalent in the minds of local people was that the killer was in their midst; a neighbour, maybe a friend, perhaps someone living just across the road. Wherever he lived, though, the fact remained that he was still at large. In fact, there was soon to be another murder.

At 9.40pm on Thursday, 31 July 1986, Robin and Barbara Ashworth, of Enderby, phoned the police to report that their 15-year-old daughter, Dawn, had not returned home from visiting friends in the nearby village of Narborough. Dawn Ashworth was a pupil at Lutterworth Grammar School, the same school as Lynda Mann. Earlier that day, she had finished her holiday job at the newsagent's at 3.30pm and called in briefly at home. She told her parents she was going to visit a couple of friends in Narborough but would be back by 7.00pm, as the couple had arranged to go out that evening. She walked to Narborough via a secluded footpath called Ten Pound Lane, near to the M1 motorway. Neither of her friends had been at home, so Dawn set off to return home at 4.30pm which, in July, was still broad daylight.

At first light on 1 August, police launched a full-scale hunt, first searching the Ashworth's family home, then initiating house-to-house enquiries between the two villages and tracker dogs combed the area. Local papers pointed out similarities between the two cases. Dawn had vanished not far from where Lynda was found, and they were the same age.

Because of the close proximity to the site of Lynda's murder, it seemed extremely unlikely that they were unconnected. The three villages close to each other lie six miles from Leicester. The Carlton Hayes Psychiatric Hospital neatly divides the villages of Narborough and Enderby and, at either end of the hospital grounds, are the two public footpaths – Black Pad to the west and Ten Pound Lane to the east.

The next day, on 2 August, the local paper carried pleas by Dawn's parents and the police for her suspected abductor to get in touch, but it was all to no avail. Later that day, police searchers found Dawn's blue denim jacket close to the motorway footbridge not far from Ten Pound Lane. That same morning, they found her body in a field flanking the lane. Her body had been hidden in a clump of bushes by piling foliage and freshly mown hay over her. She was naked from the waist down, her knickers caught on her ankle and her bra pushed up to expose her breasts. She lay on her left side in a foetal position.

That same evening, the post-mortem was carried out. Again, there were no broken fingernails and the cause of death was manual strangulation, possibly with a judo-type stranglehold from behind. There was blood evident around the vaginal area and she may have been sexually assaulted. Once these details were made public, there was very little doubt in the minds of the police, the press and the villagers that both murders had been the work of the same man.

Superintendent Tony Painter, who headed the Police Mobile Reserve Unit carrying out house-to-house enquiries during the Lynda Mann investigation, was in charge of the 200-strong murder inquiry team.

An incident room was set up by the entrance to Ten Pound Lane and police videoed a reconstruction, involving a young policewoman, dressed in clothes similar to Dawn Ashworth, retracing her route from Narborough to the lane, in an attempt to jog people's memories.

Two subsequent reports came to light. One of a young man who dashed across the M1 motorway at around 5.30pm and a man seen by two witnesses crouching in a hedgerow not far from the murder site. The most persistent reports were of a motorcyclist in a red crash helmet, seen by several witnesses, close to the footbridge across the motorway between 4.30pm and 5.30pm on the day of the murder. Although police appealed for information, these people failed to come forward and police wasted invaluable time chasing up the sightings, which led to nothing.

Police were well aware that the two crimes, which came to be known as the Enderby Murders, could be connected; there was plenty of circumstantial evidence available to suggest that connection.

Both victims were teenage girls of the same age from the same school. Both were walking along secluded footpaths. The modus operandi of the killer was similar in both cases.

Both girls had been semi-stripped, assaulted and strangled. But, most important of all, the two victims had been walking within a few hundred yards of each other, with a hospital situated between them, flanked by the villages of Narborough and Enderby and the M1 motorway. The two footpaths, Black Pad and Ten Pound Lane ran virtually parallel and were within sight of each other.

However, despite the exhaustive investigations by the police and the huge variety of witness statements, the second murder did not lead to any conclusive line of enquiry. Here was a killer who could snatch a victim in broad daylight – and not be witnessed by anyone.

On 8 August 1986, police decided to arrest 17-year-old Richard Buckland, who was employed as a kitchen porter at the Carlton Hayes Psychiatric Hospital. His name had come to the attention of the police several times throughout the course of both murder investigations. At the time of the first murder, Buckland had been 14 years old, and was well known locally as something of an oddball, big for his age, who would often jump out on women and girls and frighten them to amuse himself. Although he was originally questioned by a police officer at the time of Lynda's murder, he was not considered a likely suspect.

After Dawn's body had been found, police officers noticed him sitting astride his motorcycle watching the proceedings as police had sealed off the entrance to Ten Pound Lane.

At 9.20pm on 3 August, the day after Dawn's body had been found, he told officers he had seen Dawn walking near the footpath on the day of the murder. On Thursday, 7 August, a hospital employee told the police that

Buckland had told him that Dawn had been found hanging from a tree close to the M1 bridge in a hedge near a gate. Buckland had related this to his colleague the day before Dawn's body was discovered. So the following day, after his colleague had informed the police of this, police went to his house at 5.00am, roused him from sleep, waited until he had dressed and took him in for questioning at Wigston Police Station.

Police learned that the young man had an early history of sexual disturbance. According to people who knew him, he liked to talk about deviant sex and referred to girls as 'slags', 'dogs', 'whores' and 'bitches'. His former girlfriend told police that he liked his sex rough. He used to slap her and bite her viciously, calling her names all the while and had a preference for anal sex. Police realised that he fitted the psychological profile of the killer very well.

However, when police began to question Buckland, there came a rather bizarre twist to the murder investigation. During interviews, he would sometimes give straight answers, then contradict them, suddenly claiming he couldn't remember what had happened, and begin a description of something which was patently irrelevant. His first story recounted how he had met Dawn on the day of the murder, as she walked near the motorway bridge. Although he was about to stop for a chat, his motorbike had an oil leak so he returned home. Then he changed his story, claiming he had stopped under the bridge. He denied telling his colleague about where Dawn had been found, claiming that his colleague had told Buckland about the discovery. He then described a man with a stick who had followed Dawn and him as they chatted.

When detectives showed him a photograph of Dawn, he described how he had struggled with her and could not remember what exactly had happened next. Then, just as they were getting somewhere, he retracted all of his previous statements. Despite the inconsistencies, the story was becoming closer to the actual events and, as time went on, detectives began to feel that Buckland was their man. Eventually, he gave a clear account of overpowering the teenager, suffocating her, then having sex with her. He described how he hid her body in undergrowth which tied in with where and how she was eventually found. Again, there were denials, inconsistencies and contradictions, but the case appeared to become stronger all the time.

On Saturday, 9 August, he signed a typed statement about his version of events, pointing out the main incriminating points. In addition, he also told of other attacks unrelated to the murders. He told senior Detective Superintendent Tony Painter that, on two occasions, he had sexually assaulted a nine-year-old girl. However, despite his confession to the murder of Dawn Ashworth and details of attacks on other girls, Buckland flatly denied any involvement with the murder of Lynda Mann.

At around this time, there was a big story in the media about a geneticist who had discovered what he termed 'genetic fingerprinting'. It had taken Dr Alec Jeffreys two years to fully develop his discovery, which meant that each person could be individually identified from something as simple as a sample of their blood, semen, saliva or a hair follicle. Both the police and Buckland's father – who was convinced of his son's innocence – claimed they approached the scientist to ask for his help in drawing up what would come to be known as a DNA profile of the killer. The end result made legal history.

Dr Jeffreys tested a blood sample from Buckland and a semen sample recovered from both murder victims. The results proved beyond a shadow of a doubt that Richard Buckland had been innocent of both rapes and, in all probability, the murders, too. However, analysis of the samples from the two murders produced an identical DNA profile, proving that the killer had been responsible for both fatalities.

Although Buckland's murder trial had been scheduled to begin at Leicester Crown Court on 21 November 1986, it was cancelled, and he became the first murder suspect in legal history to be freed on the basis of his own DNA profile.

The police knew they had lost their prime suspect – yet they remained optimistic, for they now had a powerful new forensic technique to help them solve this and any other murder cases. The investigation was reopened on 2 January 1987, as the murder inquiry had gained a new direction.

DCS David Baker had come up with an idea, and gathered his detectives around him, saying, 'We're going to try something that's never been done – test every young man's blood in the three villages. All 5,000 of them.'

It was a brave decision. The test was complicated and, for each person, it would cost £120. The total cost of testing 5,000 men would be over half a million pounds. Letters requesting blood and saliva samples were sent out to the 5,000 men who fell within the police's parameters of the search for the killer – all qualifying male residents who lived locally, as well as men who had worked in the villages during the relevant periods, or who had been attending the Carlton Hayes Psychiatric Hospital as day-care patients. Two test centres were set up, each of which was manned by five doctors, working three evenings and one morning each week.

The blood and saliva samples were sent to the Forensic Science Service Laboratory in Huntingdon. Any donor who turned out to be PGM 1+ Group 'A' Secretor would have his sample sent on for DNA profiling at the FSS lab in Aldermaston. Teams of detectives researched further afield to contact men in the target age group, who used to live locally but had since moved away from the area. By the end of that month, 1,000 donors had voluntarily helped. By the third week in April, 4,195 had given blood, of whom 3,556 had been eliminated from the inquiry. Almost 5,000 men had been tested and the gamble had not yet paid off.

When all the sampling had been completed, the police were hopeful that the DNA profile would provide a match – but their optimism was short-lived. All the swabs and samples had been analysed by police forensics and no match was found. Six months after the mass screening had begun, police drew a blank. They knew that what they needed was a stroke of luck, a miracle, perhaps, that would give them a break in their investigations.

On 18 September, a Leicester policeman, whose father ran a pub called The Clarendon, phoned the murder team with the news that they had been waiting for. He had been contacted by the manager of a local bakery, Mrs Jackie Foggin, who had an interesting story to relate.

Six weeks earlier, on Saturday, 1 August 1987, she had gone to The Clarendon for lunch with a number of employees from the bakery. They sat around chatting and, eventually, the subject turned to the unsolved murders and the mass screening. Ian Kelly, one of the bakery workers, a slightly built young man with a thin moustache, told Mrs Foggin and the others that he had taken the blood test on 27 January that year, as a favour to a friend, Colin Pitchfork, by replacing his friend's passport photograph with a photo of himself.

Mrs Foggin spent six weeks agonising over what to do with this information. She did not want to get Kelly into trouble but considered that she might hold the key to the murders, so she contacted the son of The Clarendon's landlord, whom she knew was a police officer.

As soon as the murder squad detectives were informed of the identity swap, they compared the signature given by Pitchfork in the house-to-house enquiries during the investigation into Lynda Mann's murder to the signature supplied by the man claiming to be Colin Pitchfork at the mass screening. The signatures did not match.

On 19 September, police arrested Kelly at his home and he readily confessed to the deception. He explained how Pitchfork had told him that he had taken the test for another man who had a history of sexual offences and was afraid of the police. So Pitchfork forged his own passport, replacing it with a photo of Ian Kelly. On the day of the test, Ian Kelly was ill with fever, so Pitchfork picked him up at his home, drove him to the test centre and waited for him outside in the car park. Kelly was charged with attempting to pervert the course of justice and eventually received an 18-month sentence, suspended for two years.

Kelly had been an apprentice to Colin Pitchfork at the bakery and, although it later transpired that the latter had approached other colleagues at the bakery and offered them money to take the test for him, Kelly had agreed to help his friend out of trouble without payment. Kelly had only worked at the bakery for six months, having been apprentice-trained at college, and was eager to help out Pitchfork in any way he could, without the thought of profit.

Kelly was impressed by his new colleague's skills at cake decorating and set about learning as much as he could from him. As the plan for the deception matured, Pitchfork carefully coached his young friend, giving him answers to the questions that the police might ask to verify his identity, including the names of his children, their dates of birth and his wife's maiden name. He cut out his own passport photo and replaced it with Kelly's, inserting it in the space with clear sealant. A few days after the test, Pitchfork received a letter from the police informing him that his test had been negative and that he was eliminated from the inquiry.

Following Ian Kelly's arrest and explanation, the decision was made to arrest Pitchfork. When they found he was not at home, police put his house under surveillance. When they observed him returning home, they made their approach, taking care to send police officers to the rear of the house in case he attempted to escape. When he answered the door, a detective told him, 'From our enquiries, we believe you are responsible for the murder of Dawn Ashworth on 31 July 1986. We believe another man has given a blood sample for you. I am arresting you on suspicion of that murder.'

Pitchfork remained calm. 'Give me a few minutes to tell my wife.'

'Why Dawn Ashworth?' asked the detective.

Pitchfork shrugged nonchalantly. 'Opportunity. She was there and I was there.'

They accompanied him into the living room to confess to the murder to his wife, Carole; she tried to attack him and had to be held back by the police. Before they even left the house, Pitchfork also confessed to the rape and murder of Lynda Mann.

After his arrest, detectives questioned the man's colleagues at the bakery. His supervisor said that Pitchfork was a good worker and time-keeper, but that he was often moody, and he was always chatting up the female employees – he wouldn't leave them alone. In fact, police subsequently uncovered Pitchfork's history of sexual offences. However, such was the number of men screened for the mass sampling that they said they had been unable to check the criminal records of everyone who took the test.

Colin Pitchfork had been considered the black sheep of a middle-class Leicester family. While his brother and sister had studied engineering and medicine at university, the young Colin had left school with no qualifications and started work at a local bakery. By the age of 20, he had been caught and convicted twice for 'flashing'. He openly confessed that he derived much pleasure from the buzz he got from exposing himself to strangers. Although he had not been abnormal as a child, he developed a number of odd sexual characteristics. Despite his convictions, everyone who knew him says that he had a genuine liking for children and met his future wife while working as a volunteer at a children's home.

Arrested one more time for flashing, his probation officer assured him that he would 'grow out' of his urge to expose himself to females. After courting for two years, he and Carole were married in 1981. He was featured in the local paper, in a story entitled 'COLIN TAKES THE CAKE', in which he had made a birthday cake in the shape of a motorcycle for a local biker. In all this time, no one suspected him of his deadly secret. By the time the story – and the photo of him standing alongside the cake – appeared in the local paper, he had already murdered Lynda Mann, though not yet Dawn Ashworth.

In the long interviews which followed his arrest, Pitchfork gave full and detailed descriptions as to how and why he had raped and murdered the two young women and, in doing so, revealed the depth of his arrogance. Those counsellors who have since met and interviewed the killer in prison have branded him a psychopath, outlining the features of such a condition: aggressiveness, hedonism and the ability to appear normal. Unlike normal people, psychopaths lack the ordinary social feelings of conscience, empathy and regret. Self-gratification is the important goal, a single-minded pursuit of achieving something, irrespective of the consequences of his actions and how they may affect the lives of other people.

A significant aspect that was emphasised during his confessions was how he blamed the victims for 'forcing' him to murder them. His inability to express remorse or responsibility for his crimes was quite unbelievable – symptomatic of the psychopath. Unlike a serial killer, who derives pleasure and satisfaction from the act of killing, Pitchfork only turned to murder because he realised he could be identified by the girls he raped, particularly after attacking them in such close-knit, rural villages.

After his arrest, he told prison counsellors about his sexual urges. 'You get that need. You go out sometimes and cover 50 or 60 miles looking for that opportunity. It's the high I needed.' And, of his treatment at the psychiatric hospital, he was dismissive of his counsellors. As with other psychopaths, he showed that he was too manipulative to allow himself to receive psychological treatment. He said of the hospital sessions, '... A waste of time ... those people are quite happy if you tell them what they want to hear ... I can't believe how easy it is to spin yarns to these people.'

In 1983, his wife became pregnant and she became undesirable to her husband. He had an affair with a young girl who was attending the same evening class in cake decoration, and he took her into his wife's bed. Pitchfork told prison counsellors, 'I got a lot of excitement from her, combined with the exciting prospect of Carole catching us.'

When the student became pregnant, Pitchfork was ready to leave his wife for her, but the girl lost the baby and he was heartbroken. Then he confessed the affair to Carole and actually expected her to feel sympathy for him because his mistress had lost his child.

At that point, she threw him out of the house but soon took him back, but Carole never felt comfortable after that, sleeping in the same bed where her husband had made love to another woman.

Eventually, they moved to Littlethorpe, where Carole's father lived. Before the move, Carole began attending evening classes to train to be a probation officer and, on the evening of 21 November 1983, her husband drove her to the class, then went prowling the streets looking for a victim to expose himself to. Having driven around the streets, he parked the car and got out, leaving his baby son in the carry-cot on the back seat.

In the road near the hospital, he exposed himself to Lynda Mann, later telling police that she had fled in fear down the Black Pad footpath. He told police that, if she had just walked past him, she would have been safe, but the fact that she escaped along the footpath to a more secluded location had excited him more. Then he claimed that she agreed to have sex with him as long as he didn't hurt her, but he realised he may be recognised by his wedding ring, earring and thinning hair, so he strangled her. After returning to his car and his baby son on the back seat, he picked his wife up from the evening class and returned home as if nothing had happened.

He gave a similar description of the second murder, which he had intended as a spontaneous flashing exercise. He saw Dawn entering Ten Pound Lane while he was riding his motorbike. He followed her on foot and ran past her, exposing himself, and she fled through a gateway, so he ran after her, raped her and strangled her from behind with a judo strangle-hold. Once again, he claimed he had killed her to ensure she couldn't identify him, then hid her body in nettles and bushes, covering it with a log.

On describing this to detectives after his arrest, Pitchfork seemed unperturbed about committing a second murder. He merely grinned at detectives and said, 'One murder or two – the sentence is the same.' One thing that the killer stressed was that he believed the victims sealed their own fates by reacting erratically to his advances. Arrogant to the end, he blamed the victims for the murders. He told detectives, 'There's rules to how I play that game [flashing]. They always have room. No matter where I exposed myself. They always have room to walk by me. It's the easiest way. You shock them. They walk by you, and then you get your exit route clear.'

He claimed that neither victim walked away from him; that Lynda ran down a footpath and Dawn fled into a field.

'The same feelings were coming back,' said Pitchfork, 'that I was in a trap again.' He bragged to detectives of the 'thousands' of victims of his flashing escapades. This was no doubt great exaggeration, though about six of these victims were later traced by police and verified his claim.

After news of his arrest was released, a teenager went to police to report her attack from Colin Pitchfork. She had been hitch-hiking home when she was picked up by Pitchfork. To all intents and purposes, he was an ordinary young man, but she had not been in the car for long before he attacked her. After fighting him off when he tried to kidnap her, she managed to leap from the vehicle and he drove off. Only Pitchfork himself will know how close the girl came to being another murder victim.

The most shocking thing Pitchfork said to the police was how he blamed the victims for their own deaths. He claimed that the rape and murders were merely incidental to his urge to expose himself to them. He wanted control of the situations but, because of their reactions, he lost control and he felt the need to regain it.

In common with all psychopaths, Pitchfork showed a total lack of remorse for the murders. His only concern was for himself. In fact, his total calmness meant that he did not betray his emotions to his family and work colleagues, which might have made them think he was hiding something. Although the prosecution at the trial identified his supreme level of self-control in remaining calm, psychiatrists realise that this was all self-centred. He felt no guilt for his crimes, not sparing a thought for his victims or their families.

At his trial, Mr Justice Cotton told him, 'The rapes and murders were of a particularly sadistic kind. Had it not been for genetic fingerprinting, you would still be at large. In this case, it not only led to the apprehension of the correct murderer, but also ensured that suspicion was removed from an innocent man.'

He pleaded guilty to both rapes and murders and received terms of life imprisonment for the murders, ten years each for the rapes, three years each for two indecent assaults and another three years for the conspiracy charge with Kelly. However, since no recommendation for a minimum sentence to be served was suggested, much to the fury of the police and the victims' families, it meant that, in theory, Pitchfork could be released after only 12 years in prison.

By recommendation of the police, the £20,000 reward money was given to Mrs Jackie Foggin, the bakery manageress who tipped off the police in regard to the deception by Kelly and Pitchfork. Had it not been for her, then Colin Pitchfork would no doubt have claimed further victims.

13

MURDER IN JERSEY

Elizabeth Newall's forty-eighth birthday was fast approaching and, despite the ill-feeling in her family, her two sons Roderick and Mark Newall had agreed to meet up for a celebration with Elizabeth and her husband, Nicholas. The meeting was planned for the evening of 10 October 1987 at their home on the beautiful island of Jersey.

Nicholas was rich. One of two brothers who had inherited money from their family, Nicholas tried his hand at many things – including writing plays and novels, none of which was accepted by publishers – but had not achieved much of anything. His brother Stephen, however, had invested wisely and ran businesses in heavy industry. Their father had made a fortune from supplying nuts and bolts to many engineering organisations and built up a huge fortune from meagre and simple beginnings.

The evening they had arranged for their family get-together had not got off to a good start the moment they arrived at the couple's favourite restaurant, Sea Crest, boasting magnificent views of the port and the Corbiere lighthouse.

A waiter recalled that the atmosphere was tense on their table, which was surprising since the couple often dined there and always seemed to enjoy themselves.

Elizabeth was unhappy about Roderick's plans to leave his four-year military career – she had always had high hopes that he would enjoy long and distinguished service. Roderick encouraged his parents to drink more and more, which Mark hated. Elizabeth raised her voice more than once, including complaining to the head waiter that her lobster was the wrong colour and Mark argued with his father about his obsession with making money in the world of finance. The management of the restaurant were not unhappy to see them leave. In fact, they were so happy to see them leave that they forgot to charge them for the lobster.

Shortly afterwards, the family of four arrived back at the couple's home – 9 Clos de l'Atlantique in the expensive port of St Brelade. This was a modest bungalow compared to their luxurious Spanish villa where they spent much of their time.

The ill-feeling did not improve when the malt whisky was opened and everyone was offered generous measures. Mark was strongly opposed to heavy drinking and, coupled with his anger at the constant bickering, he walked out, returned to his car and drove home.

Within an hour, the arguing had increased to such a level that Roderick and his father were standing face to face in front of the fire, bawling at each other. Knocked to the ground by his father in a fit of rage, Roderick had grabbed a rice-flail which he had earlier found in the attic and beat his father to death with it by the fireplace in the lounge. Blood spattered the walls, hearth and ceiling. The 56-year-old died virtually instantly from a cracked skull.

Police never discovered whether Elizabeth saw her husband fall or only witnessed his last screams, though they were able to ascertain that she fled for her life to the master bedroom, for she was found beaten to death just inside the doorway. As she lay slumped against the door, the deep gash in her head allowed the blood to soak deep into the carpet, and so profuse was the bleeding that the blood soaked right through on to the underside of the carpet tiles.

Based on the statement he made to police six years later, Roderick phoned Mark, who drove over in a red van. They had hired this from a garage near the airport, claiming that they needed it to transport a mattress from Mark's home to his previous flat and to collect a bed. Roderick claimed to have forgotten his driving licence, and had asked his father to hire the van in his name.

At the murder scene, the two brothers had to act quickly. First, they wrapped the bodies in plastic sheeting, then bound them with twine until they were well camouflaged, put them in the van and sped through the streets of St Brelade, driving north, to Greve de Lecq, a rocky beach, popular with tourists. They used to play there as children, near the stream and in the nearby woods. Halfway up the hill was The Crow's Nest, their family home, now owned by a neighbour.

Once their parents were buried, the brothers returned to

the bungalow and set to work scrubbing the carpets and walls to rid the house of any signs of violence. They used scrubbing brushes, cloths, sponges and kitchen detergents. They washed the bloodstained sheets and replaced them on the bed before they were completely dry. At 9.00am the next morning, Maureen Ellam – who, along with her husband, had bought the Newalls' old family home, The Crow's Nest – knocked on the door and left flowers for Elizabeth for her birthday. She did not expect an answer as Elizabeth was not an early riser, and she was about to leave when Roderick came to the door, saying that his parents were still asleep.

As Mrs Ellam was later to recall, he seemed dazed and his faraway looks and quick and terse replies made her feel that something was wrong as she drove back to her home after a short conversation. She thought it unbelievable that Nicholas was still asleep, even though Roderick had told her that that was the case, as his father was a regular early riser.

By 10.00am, the brothers had ensured that they had thoroughly cleaned up the bungalow and everything in it. The carpets were soaked, the walls were dripping with detergents and the bedclothes were still damp, so, when they left the house, they turned up the central heating, hoping that everything would be dry by the time they returned.

When a friend of the family, Robert Shearer, called round to the Newalls' neighbours to ask after their whereabouts, and heard that no one had seen them, he decided to investigate for himself. He entered the house via the patio in the back garden, and found the door to be unlocked. As he entered the house, he was struck by the heat. The central heating was set at maximum. The house also looked unusually tidy – Elizabeth Newall was a notoriously untidy person.

Over the week following the murder, the police had begun a Missing Persons report for the couple. Everyone who knew Nicholas and Elizabeth considered it so uncharacteristic of the couple to have suddenly vacated their home and not told friends, neighbours or their sons where they were going and when they would return. As time passed, they began to fear that they had come to some harm.

On 19 October 1987, DS Jim Adamson interviewed the brothers and a friend of their mother's in the CID interview room.

Then a Missing Persons appeal went out through newspapers, radio and TV. The brothers said they feared something had happened to them, as they often went on long walks across the local sand dunes, or that they may have been caught by the raging storm that had recently hit Jersey and may have been blown off a cliff edge. The brothers sensed that the detectives did not believe their stories and thought they knew more than they were telling, but they could find nothing to pin on the men and they kept to the same cover story that they had given after the initial stage of filing the Missing Persons report.

Although scene-of-crime officers searched the couple's bungalow in Jersey, they did not turn up any evidence, even though subsequent searches by forensic scientists sent from the mainland found traces of blood, including spots of blood on a bed sheet in Elizabeth Newall's room and another on a poker by the fireplace.

David Northcott, a leading forensic scientist, was called in from the Home Office Laboratories at Aldermaston, and spent two days examining the bungalow. At the end of this, he concluded that the Newalls had been violently murdered. Although there had obviously been an attempt by the killers to clean up the scene to remove any traces of the killings, there were still plenty of blood samples which had been missed.

The fireside rug that had always been in place was missing. In fact, it had been so soaked in Nicholas Newall's blood that it could not be cleaned and had had to be removed by the brothers. However, despite the police's constant attempts to bring the brothers back to Jersey and to interview them, hoping they would crack and confess to the crime, the mystery continued and, for several years, it seemed that the case would never be solved.

However, a police dog-handler from the mainland began scouring the valley where the bodies had been buried. It was just one of many locations which the police considered to be the likely burial site of the Newalls. Although the animal did not find the bodies, it did locate the scene of a fire where the clean-up materials, including the fireside rug, had been burned. Remains of Elizabeth's handbag, her pen and perfume bottle were retrieved, along with part of Nicholas's pipe and fragments of a book on French restaurants with comments in the margins written by Nick's mother, Sheila. The most damaging piece of evidence was a Bissell upholstery brush containing a tuft of fibre from the lounge carpet, and other fibres from the carpet of the master bedroom. These had obviously been used as part of the clean-up operation following the murder to extract fibres and hairs from the killers. Also, there were traces of J-cloths taken from the kitchen.

Detectives gave details of the discovery at a press conference, although they withheld the exact location for tactical reasons, knowing that only the killer and detectives knew where they were found – and thus the former may let this knowledge slip in conversation with the police, implicating them in the murders. Strangely, Roderick Newall turned up at the common quite out of the blue. Detectives showed no surprise that he knew where to find them.

The police found a spade which, it was later revealed, had been bought from a builder's merchants on the island. The assistant remembered a tall, fair-haired man with broad shoulders and a German accent buying spades, a tarpaulin and scalpel knives a few days prior to the couple's disappearance, and paying for them with cash, proving beyond a shadow of a doubt that this man had been involved in the murders. Unlike the other evidence, this was found at Noirmont Common, close to where the brothers asked their neighbours if they could burn some of their rubbish, on the morning after the disappearance.

When experts began sifting the ashes for clues, they found two lenses from Nicholas Newall's glasses, which his optician said were unique to him, so detectives knew they were just as good as a fingerprint. Although the police scoured the area with a type of underground radar in an attempt to trace the bodies, they were not found. They would only be recovered and given a proper Christian burial when Roderick told police of their location after his arrest.

In their frantic clean-up exercise throughout the early

morning following the murder, the brothers missed a spray of blood that had landed on some dark surfaces. Northcott found spots of blood splashed across the glass of a picture above the fireplace. From the wide distribution of the victim's blood, Northcott concluded that someone had suffered a violent and frenzied death in the room.

Not only had the blood-soaked rug been removed, but the carpet and underlay were also soaked in it, which had, no doubt, escaped the attention of the killer. Northcott said, 'At some stage, someone was lying on the carpet long enough to lose a large quantity of blood.'

The blood marks ran the whole length of the wall to the ceiling in the lounge, staining the carpet, wall and mirror. There was also a bloodstained footprint on the lounge door.

Professor James Cameron, a Home Office pathologist who was assisting Northcott's team with their examination, concluded that the weapon had been a blunt instrument.

In July 1992, then DI Jim Adamson learned from one of his contacts that Roderick had been back in the UK for the last six weeks and was heading to Dunkeld in Scotland to talk to his uncle Stephen, his father's brother. The detective immediately attempted to locate Stephen Newall to beg for his co-operation. Even though Mr Newell was celebrating his wife's sixtieth birthday at the Dunkeld House Hotel, near Perth, he still offered to help.

With permission granted from Glasgow Police to tape the conversation on their patch, Adamson raced to meet Glasgow detectives before Roderick arrived at the hotel and took up his place in the secret recording room.

They would set up a recording device in the hotel room where Roderick would meet his uncle, hopeful for a taped confession of his part in the crimes.

When Roderick arrived, Adamson and the detectives sat there, sweating, listening intently on the headphones but, after one-and-a-half hours, Roderick had only indulged Mr and Mrs Newall in small-talk. The feeling was that the confession was soon coming, and yet the police had only prepared a two-hour tape and time was rapidly running out.

Stephen Newall suggested a breath of fresh air so he and his nephew went for a walk in the grounds before returning to the hotel room. There, as the detectives resumed their vigilance, Roderick looked directly at his uncle and confessed to murdering his parents, then burying their bodies in plastic sheeting. Stephen pressed him to say exactly where the bodies were located, but Roderick refrained from divulging such information. However, Roderick did point out that he would commit suicide if he thought there was a chance of being caught, as he did not relish the idea of spending the next 25 years of his life in a prison cell.

The detectives realised that they now had some of the strongest evidence on tape that would almost certainly lead to a secure conviction, but Adamson did not want to arrest Newall as he left the hotel that day. He intimated that he was driving to see a friend in London and, as he had not yet disclosed the location of his parents' bodies, the detective thought that he may yet confess their whereabouts.

Adamson arranged to meet the Attorney General of Jersey and play him the taped confessions, to see if he thought there may be any doubt whether they might be used as evidence against Roderick in court. After listening to the tapes, it was concluded that they were some of the best evidence of a confession ever caught on tape and so the Attorney General issued a warrant for the arrest of Roderick Newall for the murder of his parents.

But Roderick had disappeared. Even though his description was circulated to every police force in the country, as well as Interpol, he was nowhere to be seen. However, the second part of the operation was put into action. Mark Newall, suspected to be Roderick's accomplice, was coming to London. He would stay in a hotel in South Kensington, called Blake's, where he had stayed many times before. They bugged his telephone lines to record any communications. Also, as they had done with Roderick, they wanted a recent photograph of Mark to see if he had changed his appearance in the years since the murder, so they could also circulate his description to police forces if need be. So a plain-clothes officer with the Metropolitan Police secretly photographed him as he checked into the hotel.

The phone call which the police recorded was between Mark and the airline reservation desk. Mark was to fly from Heathrow to Paris, Paris to Madrid, then Madrid to Tangier, and arranged to meet his brother there.

Detectives phoned abroad and pleaded for co-operation from the authorities in Tangier to keep their eye out for Roderick's boat the *Austral Soma*, and to see if it left the port. When it did, the Ministry of Defence and the Royal Navy agreed to keep two vessels on standby to locate and close in on Newall's cruiser. The HMS *Argonaut* of the Royal Navy was put on standby to intercept Roderick's boat as it sailed out of Moroccan waters.

After many hours of scouring the waters, the detectives and seamen aboard the *Argonaut* sighted the cruiser. Armed police hid in the boat as the Captain radioed across to Newall, under the pretence of asking him whether he could come aboard for a routine check of his documents. After a long pause, Newall radioed back and agreed. He sculled across from his cruiser to the HMS *Argonaut* in a rowing boat. When he arrived on board the *Argonaut*, he was greeted by the Captain and led across the flight deck. As Newall turned the corner, he found six armed men pointing their guns at him, which took him aback. As they did not have anything resembling a cell on board the *Argonaut*, he was handcuffed to a banister and watched by an officer at all times. All the while, he raged and shouted at the guards and, as he later told police, he had been trying to work out how many officers he could kill before they shot him dead. He had also told his uncle Stephen that he would rather commit suicide than spend the rest of his life in prison, so now that he was arrested it made no odds to him how long he lived and would take every chance available to him either to retaliate, escape or die.

While Roderick was held in the prison in Gibraltar, before being extradited for trial in Jersey, his lawyers struck up a deal with police, a deal which, it was later to be stated by a senior detective on the case, was 'not worth the paper it was written on' in a legal sense. Roderick said he would offer a full confession to the double murder on the understanding that his brother Mark would only be charged as an accomplice, rather than for the murders themselves.

With this agreement in place, both men were then extradited; Roderick from Gibraltar and Mark from France, where he had since been arrested and detained. Before the plane had even touched down in Jersey, Roderick's lawyer had handed one of the detectives a small map of Greve de Lecq where Roderick said he had buried the bodies of his parents. A larger version was then drawn up and the marks were transferred to it.

Over a period of several days, Roderick Newall was escorted from La Moye Prison in Jersey to Greve de Lecq. A six-acre area had been cordoned off by police, partly because they did not know the exact location of the bodies but also to keep the press at bay, as they loitered on the perimeter with cameras and binoculars, scrutinising the tiniest movement by detectives and the prisoner, Roderick Newall, handcuffed to an officer. Although he appeared to be sincere in his attempts to recall the exact spot, Roderick did have some trouble remembering. After all, a lot of the landscape had changed in six years. Much of the earth had been landscaped by an architect, with grass, trees and mounds of earth covered with turf and replaced.

After DI Adamson had completed his testimony in court, he hurried over to Greve de Lecq where police were still searching. A mechanical digger had replaced the manual diggers and had now dug out two long thin trenches of earth revealing nothing. Adamson wondered aloud why they had not dug another trench on the other side, and suggested that they should do so. Many of the officers remained unconvinced and considered it a probable waste of time, so, as the entourage moved away, Adamson, a police constable and the digger driver set to work on the specified spot. Soon after, the digger hit rock and, beneath that, a black plastic liner was found containing what was believed to be the remains of a shoe. The digger kept pulling soil out of the hole until something bigger could be seen poking out of the earth. A pathologist on hand was called over and soon jumped into the hole with the growing numbers of police appearing at the side and looking down. Two large sheets of tarpaulin were discovered and, peering in, he concluded that there were, indeed, two bodies wrapped inside.

Identifications had to be made, but this was a mere formality. The police and the press knew it was inconceivable that the bodies could be anyone else. Examinations were made and the results disclosed during the trial some weeks later, when the dental records were compared to the remains of the bodies, as they had been examined on the evening of their discovery at the local hospital mortuary.

Roderick and Mark sat silently and impassively in the dock, as their lawyers relayed their words to the hearing. As agreed back in Gibraltar, Roderick pleaded guilty to murder and Mark pleaded guilty as an accessory to murder. Statements given by both men and read consecutively by a detective in court gave new insights into the committing of the murders, though whether these were entirely true or perhaps fabrications by the brothers to deny premeditated and cold-blooded murder of their parents is for the reader to decide.

Through his lawyer, Roderick stated that, during an argument between himself and his father, the latter hit Roderick, who fell to the floor, banging his head on a table. Enraged by this, he grabbed a rice-flail which was lying on the table and beat his father over the head with it. Some time later, he found himself sat on the hall carpet, dazed and confused. He went into the lounge to find his father dead and then, looking for his mother, also found her just inside her bedroom on the floor also beaten to death with the rice-flail. It was only then, claimed Roderick, that his temporary amnesia had lifted and he clearly recalled killing his father in a rage, and then followed suit with his mother.

Through his lawyer, Mark said that, after the family had returned to the bungalow following the restaurant meal, the arguments had continued and, still sober, Mark had walked out and driven home. A few hours later, he had received a phone call from his brother saying that he had got into a drunken rage and killed his father and mother. After immediately driving over, Mark had found Roderick sitting on the sofa with a shotgun ready to shoot himself; he was about to do this, but Mark told him they would cover up the murder together, clean up the house and bury the bodies.

After the confessions, a few expert witnesses were called, such as forensic scientists, confirming that the bodies were indeed Nicholas and Elizabeth Newall, though they had little further to add. Sentencing would take place at a later date but, for now, the detectives could relax – the case was over. Here was the result that Adamson and the other detectives had often wondered they would ever achieve. Six years after the murders, after chasing up every new lead, having had their hopes dashed at every point by quirks of fate and bad luck, their doggedness and determination had eventually been rewarded. Adamson remembers the time when he had peered down into the impromptu grave at Greve de Lecq and felt the full satisfaction of having the case come to a conclusion. At the end of the trial, though, he was enjoying a lengthy holiday in Florida with his family and was told of the good news in a phone call from a colleague who had been present in court.

But the question remains: was this an improptu attack? Did Roderick really just happen to get into an argument and murder his parents and then really regret it for the rest of his life?

Certain features of the double murder suggest that this is not the case.

Who, for example, was the man reported to have walked into the island's largest builder's merchants just days before the murder and ordered a decidedly odd list of items – so odd that the shop assistant remembered this long after the event?

The order consisted of six heavy-duty plastic sacks, two large tarpaulins, two spades, a pick-axe, a bow saw, a length of rope and a box of scalpel knives. Identical copies of most of these were recovered by the police when the bodies were found. The man paid for the order in cash rather than cheque or credit card – totalling just over £100 – arguably to avoid disclosing identification details which could later be traced back to the brothers. The spade found at Noirmont Common was definitely the same one as that on the list of purchased items.

Police made appeals in the early days of the investigations to identify this man, all to no avail. Although the man's accent sounded to the assistant as German, the description fitted that of Roderick Newall.

Also, why did the brothers hire the red van? The explanation given was that they wanted to remove a mattress from the house and hired the van as transport. Nicholas Newall ended up paying for this on his credit card and, as the prosecution counsel stated during the subsequent trial, 'Nicholas Newall was unwittingly to hire his own hearse,' as the van was used to transfer the bodies from the murder site to the burial ground.

Even when Roderick confessed to the murder to his uncle, he said he would like to meet his parents in the afterlife – but was certain it was not with the intention of apologising for his actions.

An early schoolfriend recalled how he had asked Roderick why on earth he had aspirations to join the Army, rather than move into Mark's jet-set world of big business and big money. Roderick had turned to him coolly and said, 'So that I can kill people.'

And yet, despite the notion that the murders were premeditated, why did Roderick use rice-flails as the murder weapons? They caused blood from his victims to be splashed across the carpet, walls and ceilings of the house – much of which was still evident when the forensics team embarked on the examination of the murder scene. If the murder was premeditated, why weren't the victims shot or strangled, which would certainly have left far fewer forensic clues, perhaps leaving the brothers free for the rest of their days, rather than being condemned to imprisonment?

Long after the trial and the sentencing of the brothers, the remaining members of the Newall family are attempting to redirect Nicholas and Elizabeth's fortune away from the brothers to benefit a more deserving benefactor.

The double murder remains one of the most horrific

ever known, partly because it was a case of patricide and matricide – the murder of one's parents – and partly because of the bloodshed discovered by the forensics experts, though the full reasons behind it will probably never be known.

14

MURDER INC

The East End of London has always had a rather chilling reputation, a place where gangsters ruled with an iron fist. This would certainly be true of the East End during the sixties and seventies, when the likes of the Kray twins and the Richardson Gang operated a series of underworld businesses, consisting of illicit drinking dens, protection rackets and gambling operations. And the foundation for all of these illegal businesses was the continued threat and application of extreme violence and death. The area was renowned for the reputation of its gangsters who modelled themselves on the 'Dons', who ran the crime families of America. The underworld even had its own perverse code of conduct, which precluded criminals from hurting women and children and prevented its followers from passing on information to the police regarding the activities of other offenders.

It was among these mean streets that Henry J McKenny was born and raised, learning, as many did in the East End, how to profit from crime and how to use his fists to get by. Standing some 6ft 5in tall and weighing 17 stone, he was physically imposing and a force to be reckoned with. During his early days, he made his illicit gains from petty crimes, but soon moved on to more daring and rewarding jobs. Over a short period of time, McKenny gained a reputation as a specialist in the area of robbing warehouses and business premises. During these raids, night watchmen would be terrorised into submission and the goods taken. Anyone who resisted the gang of robbers would be beaten with baseball bats or similar. Guns had not yet become the weapon of choice for the mid-ranking career criminal.

McKenny's reputation was, however, growing among the rank and file of the underworld; other criminals admired his cool nerve during robberies, while those higher up the pecking order admired his sheer size and fighting ability. McKenny would be a useful recruit as hired muscle for any of the East End gangs.

McKenny was, however, a little more than he appeared. Clearly a man with a penchant for violence and more than capable of dishing it out, he was also a man of high intelligence and possessed an extremely high IQ. Among his other notable assets were his film-star good looks and his ability as a boxer. McKenny, or 'Big Harry' as he was known, could have turned his hand to almost any trade and be expected to do well. He was a pilot and an experienced frogman but, ultimately, he chose crime, as it was easier and more lucrative.

With a blossoming reputation, it was not long before he

caught the attention of the Kray twins, Ronnie and Reggie, who both had respect for him. They extended the offer of a position with the Firm but he was able to decline them without causing offence, such was the growing status of the man.

McKenny's reputation had not just caught the attention of the Krays, the police, too, were also now keen to curtail his activities. McKenny had been inside for the odd minor infringement, but had now been arrested and convicted for a more substantial robbery and was placed under lock and key once again. It was during this period of incarceration that McKenny formed a relationship with another criminal, a relationship that would ultimately blossom into murder.

John Childs was a petty criminal – and not a very successful one at that. A weak man by character, he was very much a follower, not a leader. He was the type who could easily fall under the spell of a more dynamic and dominant individual. In due course, Childs would use this as part of his defence, blaming his own involvement in murder on McKenny's domineering hold over him.

Childs was, at the time, some way through a sentence for burglary and was sharing a cell with a man called Terry Pinfold, a hardened criminal and business partner of McKenny's. It was through this relationship that McKenny and Childs met and subsequently formed a bond, more of criminal convenience than of true friendship. During their stay with the prison service, they discussed how they might make a bit of money together once they were back in the land of the free.

Once all three were released, they got together and formed a burglary syndicate, intending to make as much money as they could in the shortest possible time. As a cover, McKenny and Pinfold also ran a legitimate business selling diving equipment; it was moderately successful, and sufficient to provide a small cover of respectability. A testament to McKenny's intelligence, he also invented a new air pump which is still in use by divers today all over the world. Whether he was ever able to exploit the business potential of his idea is not known. What is known is that he certainly loved the career path he had chosen. McKenny and Pinfold ran the business from a warehouse in Goodmayes, Essex, an address that would later become infamous.

During this period, the criminal trio planned and carried out a variety of jobs, from robbing warehouses to hijacking trucks, and they had soon introduced guns to their operation. By now, McKenny was known and feared throughout London's underworld; he was not someone you would want to cross and was feared by many for his hammer-like fists which he would use at the slightest provocation. However, they faced a problem that was quite irritating, especially to McKenny. The police were now pursuing them over every robbery and hold-up that occurred in the London area. If they had been responsible for all of the crimes they were questioned about, they would have been rich men indeed, but the truth was that their own jobs were being limited by the amount of attention the police were paying them.

It was during a conversation between McKenny and Childs one day, when McKenny was complaining about being constantly questioned by the Flying Squad every time an armed robbery occurred, that he suddenly said, 'It would just be easier to do people in for money,' and so it was that London's Murder Inc was born and the two robbers moved into the world of assassination as hit-men.

The first contract the two men carried out was murder plain and simple, and was instigated by themselves or, more rightly, by McKenny. It was not commissioned by a paying customer, but was for their own gain. McKenny and Pinfold were using a warehouse, part of which was sub-let to a soft-toy manufacturer called Terence 'Teddy Bear' Eve. While sharing the warehouse premises, McKenny could not help but notice how much money Eve was making out of his venture. It occurred to McKenny that, if Eve were removed, it would not be difficult for him and Childs to simply move in and take over the business and help themselves to the profits.

McKenny now used his intellect for the purpose of wiping out Eve. He was quite meticulous when planning, a character trait much admired by villains who did not want to go to prison. Having established how he would kill Eve, he then planned the disposal of the body or, more appropriately, the complete removal of the body. No body ... no murder. McKenny had decided to shred the body completely into tiny pieces and, to this end, prepared a slaughter house in an old East End flat, fully equipped with an electric meat-mincing machine which he had bought specially for the task from the local *Exchange and Mart*. And so the scene was set.

Eve had a regular habit of returning to the warehouse in the early evening to take care of paperwork, and it was in August 1974, when Eve once again drove back to the warehouse, that McKenny and Childs had hidden themselves in the premises while they waited for the unsuspecting victim. Eve entered the premises and walked towards a small office at the back of the warehouse. Once there, he started to remove his jacket and it was then that the two killers pounced. McKenny, armed with a length of heavy pipe studded with steel nuts, began raining blows down on Eve, who collapsed to the floor, covering his head and body. Childs then joined in, aiming blows at the poor man's head. Eve put up a brave struggle as the attackers failed to deliver the killer blow and the offensive lasted a further ten minutes before Eve was sufficiently subdued for McKenny finally to strangle him.

In line with their detailed plans, the two murderers now spent the remainder of the evening cleaning up the murder site, using sulphuric acid to remove all signs of the bloodstains. When the two were satisfied that the scene was completely sanitised, they placed Eve's body in the boot of a car and drove it round to Childs's flat in Dolphin House on Poplar High Street. The fact that the body was removed to Childs's residence, an act that would set off alarm bells in the minds of most criminals, is perhaps a clue as to the unequal partnership the two men shared.

Eve's body was discreetly carried into the building where the two men set about dismembering him. Once they had cut up the body into smaller pieces, they then fed them through the mincer and into plastic bags. Later, Childs would recall that the mincer would occasionally jam and McKenny would have to unblock the machine by poking the bits of flesh and bone out of the small holes. Finally, the machine jammed for good and so they decided to burn the remaining larger pieces.

After two days, they were left with a pile of dust and a few charred bones. The minced body parts, along with the bones, were then disposed of in a canal, while the cremated bits were scattered out of the car window while they were driving along the A31. It had been a long process, but the two were quite satisfied that they had completely covered their tracks.

The murderous pair's next victim was, unfortunately for them, linked to the killing of Eve. An ex-professional wrestler named Robert Brown and a friend of Eve's had apparently come round to the warehouse and caught McKenny and Childs in the process of a complete clean-up. Brown was a criminal himself and was on the run from the law after breaking out of Chelmsford Prison, and was looking for some assistance. When Eve failed to show up and his family became concerned, Brown became suspicious of McKenny and indicated so. McKenny put the 'frighteners' on Brown and made it clear that, if he mentioned his suspicions to the police, he would pay a heavy price. Brown was eventually apprehended and returned to prison where he kept his word and remained silent. McKenny, however, could not relax knowing that Brown could, at any time, use the information against him, either as revenge or as a bargaining tool with the authorities. It was then that he concluded that Brown, too, must die in order to guarantee the silence they both required.

He had decided to wait for Brown to be released but their opportunity presented itself sooner than they had planned when Brown, once again, escaped from the prison and actually sought out McKenny, looking for a bolt-hole. Brown was told to go to Childs's flat where he would be able to lie low for a couple of days. As Brown entered through the front door, McKenny aimed his revolver and fired three shots that hit Brown in the face and head. Once again, however, their target refused to go down easily and he fought for his life. Childs, on standby, hit Brown on the skull with a fireman's axe and then stabbed him in the chest with a knife. Still writhing on the floor, though, Brown was eventually killed when McKenny rammed a sword through him, effectively pinning him to the floor. Again, the two men set about dismembering the body, putting the pieces into the fireplace, where they were burned.

Up to this point, McKenny and Childs had not yet been paid as hit-men and were now actively touting for business. The word was put out among the London underworld that a hit could be arranged for a suitable pay-off, and McKenny even touted his murderous service to the family of Lord Lucan.

However, their first paid assignment was just around the corner. George Brett was a tough East End haulage contractor, a man on the fringes of the London underworld and who was not averse to punching it out with the best of them. In October 1973, Brett got involved in an almighty fight with another man who moved in criminal circles. The fight had been a good match until Brett produced an iron bar and began pummelling his opponent to the ground. Brett inflicted such serious injuries that the man nearly died, a mistake he would come to regret bitterly.

The man made a slow recovery in hospital, harbouring a major grudge and planning to extract his own vengeance when the time was right. The man concerned had heard of McKenny and Childs's services as hit-men and decided to take them up on their offer, paying £1,800 to have Brett killed. On the pretence of doing some business as a haulage contractor, Brett was lured to the warehouse in Goodmayes, where he was to meet a 'Mr Jennings', who was, in reality, Childs. Brett, however, had his suspicions regarding the meeting and had always been wary of reprisals, and so decided to take his ten-year-old son Terry along as a form of insurance, believing that the underworld code advising against violence in the presence of children would protect him.

Brett, however, had underestimated the psychopathic tendencies of his killers. As Brett entered the warehouse, he was met by Childs who calmly kept him talking for a few moments while McKenny moved into position. Once within range, McKenny opened fire with a machine-gun, shooting Brett dead. Ten-year-old Terry Brett was standing only a few feet away when McKenny ordered Childs to grab the boy and to hold him still; McKenny then shot the young boy through the head. Childs would later say, 'If I'd have had a gun in my hand at that moment, I would have shot Big Harry to pieces. I could not believe he had shot the boy as well.' The crime scene was cleaned and the bodies were disposed of in their now familiar style, leaving next to nothing to be found.

Unlike Robert Brown who was still thought to be a convict on the run, Brett and his son were reported missing by his family to the police. A major search was instigated, and the missing child was of particular concern. Brett owned a number of properties around London and police systematically checked each in turn. They occasionally received anonymous tip-offs that the bodies of the two could be found in one location or another. One strong tip-off suggested that they could be found at Mount Pleasant Farm in Upminster. The police went over the area with a fine-tooth comb but could find no trace of the victims. Underworld contacts were questioned, but no one would come forward with any information that could shed any light on the disappearances.

McKenny and Childs had carried out their task efficiently and no one seemed to mention the killing of Terry Brett as a step too far. Their reputation now firmly established, they were ready once again to accept another paid assignment. The next murder was committed in July 1978, and was that of a 48-year-old nursing-home manager named Freddie Sherwood. You don't ask too many questions as a hit-man, and McKenny was more interested in the rewards than the reasons and accepted the task.

Sherwood was to be killed and this time they would receive the sum of £4,000, with £1,500 to be paid in advance and the balance to be paid in monthly instalments of £500. With the deal agreed, McKenny and Childs started to look at how they would carry out the assassination. The perfect opportunity arose when Sherwood advertised his car for sale in the local newspaper. Childs phoned Sherwood on the pretence of being interested in the vehicle. Childs then agreed to call round to Sherwood's house where he inspected the car, telling Sherwood that he was interested and that he would conclude the deal in cash if he would drive him to his house, which was, in fact, McKenny's bungalow, situated next to the now infamous warehouse.

Sherwood, who had been promised cash up front, entered the bungalow and was handed the money, which he proceeded to count while he was seated at McKenny's kitchen table. McKenny, approaching from behind, then shot Sherwood in the head and Childs proceeded to club Sherwood with a hammer until Sherwood's lifeless body lay blood-spattered on the kitchen floor. The body was then driven in the boot of Sherwood's own car to the flat in Poplar, where, once again, the body was taken apart and burned in the fireplace.

When the police received reports of Sherwood's disappearance, they carried out the usual checks, but with no body they would not commence a murder inquiry and so Sherwood became another apparently confusing Missing Persons statistic, but one of many that occurred every year in London. Murder Inc was still, therefore, very much in business and ready for its next client.

The next case of murder would, however, be another private matter for McKenny. McKenny was having an affair with the wife of one of his friends, a man called Ronald Andrews. McKenny was quite smitten with the lady and was becoming jealous and annoyed at the ongoing relationship between Andrews and his wife. Over a period of time, McKenny started to think it would be easier for him if Andrews was out of the picture; he was as capable of killing one of his own friends as one of somebody else's. He therefore plotted to kill the roofing contractor and called Childs in for assistance, paying him £4,000 and providing him with a silencer for one of his handguns.

Childs had never met Andrews and so was able to play the stooge once again. Andrews had become suspicious that his wife was having an affair when Childs approached him as a private investigator saying he would be willing to follow the lady and perhaps find out who the 'secret lover' might be. Andrews was thinking the offer over when Childs suggested Andrews come round to the flat to discuss the case, an offer which Andrews unfortunately accepted. On arrival at the flat, Andrews was ushered inside and would have only had a few moments to register surprise at seeing McKenny there. Almost immediately, McKenny strode towards Andrews, pointing his .38 revolver at him and killing him with a deadly shot. The body was, once again, dismembered and burned in the fireplace. McKenny and Childs then drove Andrews's Lincoln Continental to the river near Wisbeck and rolled it into the water. They had placed a bottle of vodka on the passenger seat to give the impression of suicide. The windows and door to the vehicle were left open in the hope that people would believe the body had floated away down the river. A couple of days later, the car was reported by fishermen but Andrews had not even been reported missing.

The deadly duo now had a body count totalling six, and not one police question had they had to answer. The problem for them was that they had not earned the money they had hoped for and were soon planning to get involved in robbery again, only this time they intended to pull off a much bigger job, a job that would ultimately reveal to the police the lethal activities the two men had been involved in between 1974 and 1978.

McKenny and Childs now assembled a team of professional armed robbers to carry out a robbery on a cash-carrying Security Express van. The team planned to hijack the vehicle and collect the cash as the vehicle made its rounds, using an extreme threat of violence to keep the security staff under control.

The gang lay in wait and, eventually, got one of the guards at gunpoint, forcing the other, who was locked in the van, to let the other members of the team on board. The guards were then told to continue on their cash collection rounds as normal. At each stop, the guard leaving the vehicle to collect the cash was reminded that, if he didn't comply with the group's instructions, the guards left on the van would be shot with the guns that were being openly brandished. The guards carried out their instructions to the letter and the team were soon in possession of half a million pounds in used notes.

As the operation was now coming to a close, the team instructed the van driver to head for a public toilet in a quiet area. Here, the guards were tied up and the team removed the grey boiler suits they had been wearing for the raid, discarding them in the public convenience. As the daring crew made their escape the police arrived at the toilets, alerted by a member of the public, and began to question the guards and examine the clothing the gang had foolishly left behind. In the pocket of one of the boiler suits, the police found a BMW car key, which enquiries showed belonged to a man called Philip Cohen. Cohen was arrested and questioned about the crime, in which he could not deny his involvement. In a bid for leniency, Cohen named the other members of the gang, who were all easily rounded up, including Childs. McKenny, however, managed to avoid capture and went on the run.

Cohen, another weak criminal, and out of his depth on the security van heist, was now so desperate to avoid a long stretch in prison that he had additional information, much more important than his accomplices in the robbery. The police assured Cohen that any help he was able to provide would help his cause when he finally came up in front of the judge, and so Cohen said, 'Johnny Childs and Big Harry have been committing murders for years.' The police listened with great interest as first Cohen, then other members of the gang, listed the names of the six individuals whom Childs and McKenny had murdered.

DCS Frank Cater, the officer in charge of the case, questioned Childs over a two-week period. Childs, too, was now providing information, and in an apparently reflective mood he became keen to clear his conscience, as the killings had been weighing heavy on his mind. Childs provided a lot of detail and backed up all of his claims, and he also provided an address where he told the police they could find a stash of his weapons. At the location, the police recovered two metal boxes containing an awesome array of weapons, six handguns, four pump-action shotguns, a telescopic sporting rifle and a Mark 2 Sten sub-machine-gun.

The police were now convinced that Childs was telling the truth and forensic evidence recovered from a number of addresses used by the two men helped to provide the additional proof. The police were now keen to arrest McKenny, who had fled to France in the aftermath of the botched robbery and had taken his girlfriend, Gwen Andrews, with him. Cater was desperate not to provoke McKenny – he was armed and highly dangerous – but the papers had now found themselves in possession of the information concerning the murders and they were keen to run the story. Cater was able to persuade the press not to run the story as a matter of public safety, hoping to avoid backing McKenny into a corner while he was spooked and ending up in the middle of a bloody shoot-out.

However, when the police made little progress, the press began to release snippets of the story, saying that the security van robbery was also linked to a number of killings. Although no one was named in the article, it would have been obvious to McKenny that his murderous past was now public knowledge. The police now felt obliged to disclose the official information and released full photos of McKenny. McKenny was reported driving a Volkswagen car in Ilford and, after a brief chase, managed to slip through the net once again.

McKenny remained free until 20 September 1979, when another tip-off led police to an address in Plaistow, East London. The police surrounded the house and then phoned the occupants, saying that the house was now surrounded by armed police. McKenny walked out and gave himself up without a struggle, where he was handcuffed and taken to Plaistow Police Station.

At trial, Childs pleaded guilty and was sentenced to life imprisonment; McKenny went into the dock in 1980 and pleaded not guilty, but his case was severely weakened when Childs became the chief prosecution witness against him and he, too, was imprisoned for life with a recommendation that he serve not less than 25 years.

During the trial, the forensic team undertook some quite bizarre experiments to provide additional evidence against McKenny. They dismembered an 11st pig to prove that it was possible to dispose of a body through a mincing machine and also by being incinerated in a normal domestic fireplace.

John Childs is still alive and is serving his sentence at

Her Majesty's pleasure in Belmarsh Prison, where he is disliked immensely by other prisoners and is regularly attacked, almost being killed two years ago by a fellow inmate who coshed Childs with a rock-filled sock.

McKenny remains a source of much mystery; we do not know which prison he is being held in, as the Data Protection Act prevents the disclosure of such information. He may, of course, by now be dead.

The two men have never expressed any remorse for their killings, although Childs did at least provide information so the families of the deceased could finally know what happened to their loved ones. McKenny and Childs finally paid a great price, far in excess of the small sums of money they were able to demand for their services, a price that finally closed the door on London's Murder Inc.